The Need For Rapid Deployment Is NOW

Boots On The Ground

Proverbs 11:30

James R. Davis, Sr.

ISBN 978-1-63903-995-1 (paperback)
ISBN 978-1-63903-996-8 (digital)

Christian Faith Publishing
832 Park Avenue
Meadville, PA 16335
www.christianfaithpublishing.com

Cover Design by Mark A. Davis I

Printed in the United States of America

ENDORSEMENTS

Dr. James R. Davis Sr. draws us back to the essential ministry and biblical calling of not only the local church but of every believer—evangelism. The mantra of our church is that we are "empowered to win souls for Christ," and I am grateful for a rare reminder of our individual and collective mission. The challenges of our time are a stark reminder for us to get back to our purpose because it is evident more now than ever that the world needs to know Jesus, and the church must be deployed to introduce Him to the world.

—RUBIN THOMPSON
PASTOR OF MORNING STAR FULL GOSPEL
ASSEMBLY, BRONX, NEW YORK

If there ever were a need for rapid deployment of the church, it's now! The obstacles we faced in 2020 required Godly wisdom, practical application, and unconditional love. *BOOTS ON THE GROUND* takes us straight to the needy as good Samaritans and not to the other side, ignoring God's will.

—RONA E. DRUMMER
LIVING BY DESIGN (TM), CONSULTANT,
RALEIGH, NORTH CAROLINA

Dr. James R. Davis Sr., thank you for an inspiring, empowering, educational, and, most importantly, a motivating book to get us up and get to work now. We can do this! Dr. Davis, you have shown us what it means to be "boots on the ground" for the kingdom of God by being our pastor, teacher, mentor, and, most importantly, an example. Now LET'S DO THIS!

—MARION AND GLORIA TAYLOR
GRIME CONTROL & RECYCLING SERVICES,
LLC, RALEIGH, NORTH CAROLINA

It is my distinct honor to endorse Dr. James R. Davis Sr., author of *THE NEED FOR RAPID DEVELOPMENT IS NOW: BOOTS ON THE GROUND*. He has proven himself to be loyal and dedicated in both his professional and personal life. Having known him for over ten years, I personally can say he is an individual who leads by example. His intellectual concepts are supported accurately with a very relaxed approach. I pray that everyone who reads this book will be blessed tremendously through spiritual growth

—CRYSTAL MATTHEW-MARROW, CFSP
OWNER OF MATTHEW FAMILY MORTUARY,
ROCKY MOUNT, NORTH CAROLINA

This opportunity only comes once in a lifetime, and I am beyond humbled to endorse the wonderful work of Dr. James R. Davis, Sr. The literature that follows speaks volumes to his unrelenting effort to honor God with his gifts of teaching and writing in such a way that God's intentions are met for His people. I have known the author since September of 2012, and I have experienced the most well-educated and traveled, patient, professional, hardworking gentleman I could ever meet. He has taught me so much over the years, and I am truly thankful for his wisdom. It is my hope that all readers of *THE NEED FOR RAPID DEPLOYMENT IS NOW: BOOTS ON THE GROUND* will initiate a new perspective, a new relationship, and a zeal for Christ Jesus and His ministry.

—RHONDA S. PITTMAN,
AGENCY DIRECTOR AND OWNER OF LIFESAVER RESOURCES,
INC., ROCKY MOUNT, NORTH CAROLINA

Powerful, riveting, and humbling. Dr. Davis has rendered the body of Christ a thought-provoking and motivating call to action. While there remains one dark soul without the light of Christ, we MUST heed the call, for the time of deployment is NOW.

—PAMELA ROGERS,
M. ED, QUEENS, NEW YORK

The Need for Rapid Deployment Is Now: Boots on the Ground and a vital tool for every "foot soldier" on today's evangelistic field.

—Wilson P. Comfort,
Owner and Operator of Comfort Enterprises, LLC.
Professional Lawncare Services, Raleigh, North Carolina
Assistant to the Pastor, Bread of Life Christian Church

Year 2020 has been a year of tremendous economic, social, and spiritual challenges encompassed with fear and death. For many, our faith has been tested. *The Need for Rapid Deployment Is Now: Boots on the Ground* inspires us to get up from sitting down and to do "the work of the church" so that the Lord's house may be filled.

—Dr. Shaniqua Council Archer
Bread of Life Christian Church and Community
Center, Inc., Rocky Mount, North Carolina

To my wife, Lorraine Sutrina Peele Davis, who for the past fifty-five years has been my anchor in encouraging me to think clearly and rationally about my relationship with God and to engage in reflective and independent thinking. Confidently, her faith in me, along with her knowledge of the God of the Bible, has allowed me to think critically. Someone with critical thinking skills can understand the logical connections between ideas. I affectionately call my wife Lady because that is who she is—an extraordinarily strong lady who acknowledges God in everything.

CONTENTS

FOREWORD

I encourage everyone who has a love for the gospel of Jesus Christ and the desire to make that love come alive in your personal life, as well in your community, to read *THE NEED FOR RAPID DEPLOYMENT IS NOW: BOOTS ON THE GROUND* by Dr. James R. Davis, Sr. Dr. Davis clearly and succinctly details why evangelism really is our *boots-on-the-ground* approach to working out our love for Christ and His Word. As Dr. Davis's neighbor and friend for more than twenty years, I have observed firsthand the application of Scripture in his daily walk and family life. A family man, hardworking citizen, and conscientious man of faith, Dr. Davis has dedicated his life to building up communities that have been devastated through disinvestment, given over to crime and hopelessness, and deserted by people who seek higher economic status. I have witnessed Dr. Davis's zeal, knowledge, and perseverance begin to transform inner-city streets into burgeoning oasis of excellence and work together with many others to bring hope through evangelism, instruction, affordable housing, and family support. Exuberance and authenticity define two of his greatest characteristics as a pastor, community servant, and man of God. *Boots on the Ground* reflect both his intellectual prowess and his love for the everyday person. Complex theological concepts are presented with clarity, simplicity, and in a manner that all of us can embrace and apply. I have read the book from cover to cover and encourage you to do the same. And now the fun part begins—putting what I have learned into practice!

REUBEN C. BLACKWELL IV
PASTOR, CORNERSTONE COMMUNITY CHRISTIAN CHURCH
PRESIDENT AND CEO, OPPORTUNITIES INDUSTRIALIZATION
CENTER OF ROCKY MOUNT, NORTH CAROLINA
CITY COUNCIL REPRESENTATIVE, ROCKY MOUNT, NORTH CAROLINA

PREFACE

We are living in a time where matters concerning the church and our personal relationships with the Creator is in conflict between our spirituality and our daily living. This book is a product of those concerns over many years of sharing the gospel of Christ on the streets of New York City, New Jersey, Connecticut, North Carolina, and writing textbooks and pamphlets for our Bible Institute, New Covenant Bible Institute, Inc., as well as ministering in various places of worship. It was birthed in my heart several years ago but never realized until this moment in time. At this most crucial time in our nation's history, our country has been affected by the coronavirus pandemic, which is consuming not only our nation but the world, and through the prompting of the Holy Spirit, God is allowing me for the very first time to write a book. At one time, I would have questioned God, but because of a better understanding as to who He is, I know that writing now is the best time because His timing is different than mine. Therefore, for the purpose of advancing the kingdom of God, always follow the leading of the Holy Spirit, for He will lead and guide us into all truth.

Evangelism has always been a passion of mine, and now, I can share why I think that the increase of the kingdom of God is not only a divine fiat from God but, rather, it is a calling and a priority that cannot be ignored by all believers in Jesus Christ. Evangelism helps to dissipate the despair we face daily by instilling within us a hope that dispel all distractions, giving us a better way of living with unlimited expectations. I hope and pray that this book will meet and answer some of the expectations of all those who read this work of increasing God's kingdom.

Observing the behavior of those who claim the salvation of Christ, I discovered that you could lie, steal, cheat, and raise all kind of H-E-double-hockey-sticks, while claiming to be anointed by God to teach, preach, and sing Zion's songs. However, if you teach, preach, and sing, make sure your lifestyle is an example to others. The definition of gross negligence on the part of many believers in Jesus Christ is when we fail to apply God's Word in our everyday activities. It is time for us to walk the walk that we have so embraced in our dialogue of talking the talk. Those of us having come to Christ must now go for Christ. As our late sister Pearl Wiggins, one of the disciples of Bread of Life Christian Church and Community Center, Inc., often articulated through one of her favorite songs (written by the late Rev. Timothy Wright), "GET ON UP FROM SITTING DOWN. GOD CAN'T USE YOU SITTING DOWN." The need for rapid deployment is now; therefore, it is imperative that we get on up from sitting down and be about our Father's business.

> TRAIN UP A CHILD IN THE WAY HE SHOULD GO [TEACHING HIM TO SEEK GOD'S WISDOM AND WILL FOR HIS ABILITIES AND TALENTS], EVEN WHEN HE IS OLD, HE WILL NOT DEPART FROM IT. (Proverbs 22:6 AMP)

> YOU CALL ME TEACHER AND LORD, AND YOU ARE RIGHT IN DOING SO, FOR THAT IS WHO I AM… SO IF, THE LORD AND TEACHER, WASHED YOUR FEET, YOU OUGHT TO WASH ONE ANOTHER FEET AS WELL… FOR I GAVE YOU [THIS AS] AN EXAMPLE, SO THAT YOU SHOULD DO [IN TURN] AS I DID… I ASSURE YOU AND MOST SOLEMNLY SAY TO YOU, A SLAVE IS NOT GREATER THAN HIS MASTER, NOR IS ONE WHO IS SENT GREATER THAN THE ONE WHO SENT HIM… IF YOU KNOW THESE THINGS, YOU ARE BLESSED [HAPPY AND FAVORED BY GOD] IF

YOU PUT THEM INTO PRACTICE [AND FAITHFULLY DO THEM]. (John 13:13–17 AMP)

LET NO ONE LOOK DOWN ON [YOU BECAUSE OF] YOUR YOUTH BUT BE AN EXAMPLE AND SET A PATTERN FOR BELIEVERS IN SPEECH, IN CONDUCT, IN LOVE, IN FAITH, AND IN [MORAL] PURITY. (1 Timothy 4:12 AMP)

The time and need for rapid deployment, an evangelistic thrust, is now. Therefore, get up from the seat of doing nothing and put into practical application all that you have learned by continuously studying the Word of God. You should also be acquainted with secular understanding from education, community and political activism, volunteerism, and your personal testimony. Likewise, be knowledgeable of the political and social structure for our cities, states, nation, and the world. Never ever forget that you have been called and ordained to cry out against any injustice, wherever it may be found. Failure to do this makes you culpable. We need boots on the ground now.

Our pilgrimage in life has been plagued with unequal opportunities in business, education, the work environment, and a multiplicity of other lifestyle choices. These areas are filled with vicissitudes which, inextricably, are geared toward distractions from your purpose and have created an atmosphere of uncertainty and confusion. The questions we are wrestling with are: "Why me?" and "Am I good enough to compete in the same areas where I am just as or possibly more qualified than my counterparts?" Be it male or female, why do available promotions seem to elude the best of us? We in the church have bypassed the secular for the spiritual only, and as a result, we have made a grave error. We forgot that God is concerned with the whole man, not just the choices that we make which seem to define us in ways some have determined is acceptable or not. Nebuchadnezzar, an ungodly and more than a qualified leader, chose the best young men of Israel to forge and promote his ungodly purposes. It did not matter whether these young men were spiritual or not; he wanted the best. And yes, the best was among those that were spiritual. Without question, there is a need for evangelistic deployment now.

Some of the following distractions that hinder our journey in life are as follows: discrimination, politics, abusive relationships, systemic racism, police brutality, unequal opportunities in education and employment. Yes, there are more distractions; however, let us focus on the few before we tackle the many. Attempting to handle the many, we overlook the little foxes that will destroy your effort in kingdom building. Knowledge of evangelistic efforts is sorely needed in our churches today.

However, for pedagogical reasons, learning concerning matter of necessity for our existence are uncomfortable moments of collective realities. Everything concerning our wherewithal becomes primary and necessary for our upward mobility to achieve the measure of success we have been working so hard to attain. First Thessalonians 5:21 (AMP) says, "BUT TEST ALL THINGS CAREFULLY [SO YOU CAN RECOGNIZE WHAT IS GOOD]. HOLD FIRMLY TO THAT WHICH IS GOOD."

Learning is the prerequisite designed to empower conscious thoughts to achieve uncommon expectations of valor. Each of us are born with certain innate qualities to render the enemy of our lives helpless. This propensity creates an atmosphere which causes one's faith to shatter the move of the ignorant that do not have the knowledge and understanding nor the ability to overcome their lack.

> I CAN DO ALL THINGS [WHICH HE HAS CALLED ME TO DO] THROUGH HIM WHO STRENGTHENS AND EMPOWERS ME [TO FULFILL HIS PURPOSES—I AM SELF-SUFFICIENT IN CHRIST'S SUFFICIENCY; I AM READY FOR ANYTHING THROUGH HIM WHO INFUSES ME WITH INNER STRENGTH AND CONFIDENT PEACE]. (Philippians 4:13 AMP)

The answer for the world, without question, is Jesus. Yet for the propagation of the Gospel message, we MUST prepare and be ready to go and declare the works of the Lord at any moment. A noteworthy comment is that the times in which we live today, answering the questions of those who have had encounters with the church in a negative way, need the church to respond to their concerns. This is a major concern when we the people of God cannot answer the reasonable questions put to them by those seeking help for the dilemma they find themselves in.

> BUT IN YOUR HEARTS SET CHRIST APART [AS HOLY—ACKNOWLEDGING HIM, GIVING HIM FIRST PLACE IN YOUR LIVES] AS LORD. ALWAYS BE READY TO GIVE A (LOGICAL) DEFENSE TO ANYONE WHO ASKS YOU TO ACCOUNT FOR THE HOPE AND CONFIDENT ASSURANCE [ELICITED BY FAITH] THAT IS WITHIN YOU, YET [DO IT] WITH GENTLENESS AND RESPECT. (1 Peter 3:15 AMP)

This vision of reaching the lost in every place on the face of this earth can only be realized when the vision can be passed on to someone else, and they begin to support it. Alone, you cannot bring the vision to pass although it was birthed in you. However, you will need someone who will catch the vision and run with it. God + Me + You can bring this vision, boots on the ground, into fruition. Now, we can go into all the world. This is the work of the church.

Achieving the planned objectives of winning souls to Christ gives us a sense of accomplishment and motivation to do the work of evangelism. Amidst failures in reaching our goals leaves many with a defeatist attitude. For every failure, it is only an opportunity to grow. Get on up from sitting down. God cannot use you sitting down.

THE NEED FOR RAPID DEPLOYMENT IS NOW.

CHAPTER 1

EVANGELISM

Go therefore and make disciples of all the nations
[help the people to learn of Me, believe in Me, and
obey My words], baptizing them in the name of the
Father and of the Son and of the Holy Spirit.
—Matthew 28:19 (AMP)

Evangelism is the proclamation of the gospel of peace. It is the good news as commanded by our Lord and Savior Jesus Christ. Evangelism emerged because of a collision or a war of two cultures that are struggling and are diametrically opposed to each other. Their view of freedom of choice is a war of conscious thought that can only be defined by what is right for me may be wrong for you. However, your thoughts are your thoughts, and my thoughts, ways, and actions belong to me. The freedom of choice allows individuals the right, with respect to lifestyle, autonomy, philosophy, etc., to make decisions for themselves. This is a war between spirituality and rationalism. The spiritual adhere to the things of God while the rational depends solely on humanistic reasoning. Kevin J. Conner and Ken Malmin, in my understanding, compare this war between two method of studies: the rationalistic and the literal methods of study.

The rationalistic method, according to Conner and Malmin, "presumes that the Bible is not the authoritative inspired Word of God. It interprets Scripture as a human document in the light of human reason." With the rationalist, nature is the standard and reason is the guide. *The literal method* assumes that the words of Scripture, in their plain evident meaning, are reliable, that God intended His revelation to be understood by all who believe, that the words of Scripture communicate what God wants man to know. The evangelist MUST understand these two methods, opposed to each other, can be used to answer questions of the hope needed to escape the pitfalls of sin.

> THE BEGINNING OF WISDOM IS: GET [SKILLFUL AND GODLY) WISDOM [IT IS PREEMINENT]! AND WITH ALL YOUR ACQUIRING, GET UNDERSTANDING [ACTIVELY SEEK SPIRITUAL DISCERNMENT, MATURE COMPREHENSION, AND LOGICAL INTERPRETATION]. (Proverbs 4:7 AMP)

Also, James 1:5 (AMP) gives additional clarity for the evangelist to us to be an effective witness for Christ: "IF ANY OF YOU LACK WISDOM [TO GUIDE HIM THROUGH A DECISION OR CIRCUMSTANCE], HE IS TO ASK OF [OUR BENEVOLENT] GOD, WHO GIVES TO EVERYONE GENEROUSLY AND WITHOUT REBUKE OR BLAME, AND IT WILL BE GIVEN TO HIM."

In our world today, there is a war going on that is constantly spreading throughout our cities, states, nations, and, subsequently, the entire world. This war is of such that the participants are willing to destroy everything and everyone in its path just to say that "I am right, and you are wrong." The battleground for this war is a place where our greatest struggles occur. This is the battleground of our human consciousness, the mind. THE NEED FOR RAPID DEPLOYMENT IS NOW.

> WRETCHED AND MISERABLE MAN THAT I AM! WHO WILL [RESCUE ME AND] SET ME FREE FROM THIS BODY OF DEATH [THIS CORRUPT, MORTAL EXISTENCE]?... THANKS BE TO GOD [FOR MY DELIVERANCE] THROUGH JESUS CHRIST OUR

LORD! SO THEN, ON THE ONE HAND I MYSELF
WITH MY MIND SERVE THE LAW OF GOD, BUT ON
THE OTHER, WITH MY FLESH [MY HUMAN NATURE,
MY WORLDLINESS, MY SINFUL CAPACITY—I SERVE]
THE LAW OF SIN. (Romans 7:24–25 AMP)

Evangelism is the act of sharing your personal encounter with Jesus, with the ultimate hope that it will convince others to accept Him as their Lord and Savior so that His kingdom on earth will increase. The work of evangelism is the proclamation of glad tidings, of our Lord and Savior Jesus Christ, shared with those not known to have accepted Him as their personal Savior. The instructions and pastoral care of those who are believers fall under the heading of SOUL WINNING. Therefore, the primary and most important task of evangelism, along with the responsibility of the believer, is to be a conduit, so impactful that it will free humanity from the bondage and curse of a sinful existence.

Now, sin is the innate quality within man to do wrong. To be perfectly clear, sin is not wrong actions although these actions are wrong by their very nature; but rather, sin is your unconverted inborn nature which thrives in acts of disobedience, which now identifies you with the proclivity to do wrong; thus, you are now known by your deeds as a sinner.

The work of the church, in every department, should be the promotion of evangelism. The importance of this work cannot and should not be ignored. The evangelist must preach and teach the love, mercy, and judgment of God. We can conclude that the first and most important principle of the church is that we, the church, is a body under orders by Christ, the Commander in Chief, to share His gospel throughout this entire world. Our biblical mandate as a body of baptized believers in Christ is to evangelize.

The most strategic, underrated, and unused key to evangelization is the layman. It is extremely and very essential to create a program which will motivate, recruit, and train every believer to follow the mandate of Christ, to go into all nations and evangelize. When we compare Acts 8:1 and Acts 8:4, we conclude, although everyone was scattered throughout the world, the apostles and the laymen were the instruments God used to carry His Word to His people. Psalm 24:1 (AMP) says, "THE EARTH IS THE LORD'S, AND THE FULLNESS OF IT, THE WORLD AND THOSE WHO DWELL IN IT." Yes, we all belong to the Lord, so let us go into all the world and preach and teach Jesus, the Savior of the world.

The multiplication method of evangelism, as I see it, will fulfill the mandates of Scripture the Lord added daily to the church such as should be saved. This is one of the best methods, if you can grasp its understanding, to grow the local assembly, subsequently, enlarging the kingdom of God. For every soul you win to Christ is a gain of one. For every two souls you win is a gain of four. Four every four you win is a gain of sixteen, etc. Since 99 percent of the church is made up of laymen, if they are AWOL, then there is a great possibility that the work of evangelism would be curtailed greatly, if not completely lost. Therefore, it is incumbent upon leaders of the church to train new believers, as well as those who missed out on proper training, in the art of evangelism to win souls to Christ. Around 95 percent of all converts never win anyone to Christ because they are not equipped to do this necessary work. Training a person to evangelize is more fruitful than inviting them to church or some special program. The soul-winning effort that is attached to evangelism will nourish, strengthen, and prepare that soul to prioritize his or her efforts in this endeavor to build up all those who, through the evangelistic thrust, accept the Lord Jesus Christ as their personal Savior, and then they too will be ready to take the gospel to the streets.

The one event that had the greatest effect in the lives of humanity also has led to an attitude of ambivalence. That is to say that something good and bad is happening at the same time, love and hate coexisting at the exact moment in time, and something extremely horrific and yet wonderful and empowering and impacting us at the same moment. This event entailed the birth, life, death, and resurrection of our Lord and Savior, Jesus the Christ. The death of Christ left an emptiness, a void, a disconnect in the lives of so many of His followers; yet from the perspective of ambivalence, His resurrection not only left a nation in despair, but it was an awakening of the hope of our eternal existence as He so promised.

> THE HOUR HAS COME FOR THE SON OF MAN TO BE GLORIFIED AND EXALTED... I ASSURE YOU AND MOST SOLEMNLY SAY TO YOU, UNLESS A GRAIN OF WHEAT FALLS INTO THE EARTH AND DIES, IT REMAINS ALONE [JUST ONE GRAIN, NEVER MORE]. BUT IF IT DIES, IT PRODUCES MUCH GRAIN AND YIELDS A HARVEST... THE ONE WHO LOVES HIS LIFE [EVENTUALLY] LOSES IT [THROUGH DEATH], BUT THE ONE WHO HATES HIS LIFE IN THIS WORLD [AND IS CONCERNED WITH PLEASING GOD] WILL KEEP IT FOR LIFE ETERNAL. (John 12:23–25 AMP)

For some, the greatest challenge they now face is one of "FAITH." After all the evidence they experienced, yet for purpose of validation, the need for additional proof loomed largely for something that they could physically touch and see. We must do our best to avoid unrealistic expectations so that our integrity is not compromised by bad decisions and poor choices.

> NOW FAITH IS THE ASSURANCE [TITLE DEED, CONFIRMATION] OF THINGS HOPED FOR [DIVINELY GUARANTEED], AND THE EVIDENCE OF THINGS NOT SEEN [THE CONVICTION OF THEIR REALITY— FAITH COMPREHENDS AS FACT WHAT CANNOT BE EXPERIENCED BY PHYSICAL SENSES]. (Hebrews 11:1 AMP)

Faith in Christ is an undeniable confidence that supersedes a performance in front of others. It is knowing without seeing, which brings glory and honor to the One who was willing to be the Substitute in death for fallen humanity.

JESUS SAID TO HIM, "BECAUSE YOU HAVE SEEN ME, DO YOU NOW BELIEVE? BLESSED [HAPPY, SPIRITUALLY SECURE, AND FAVORED BY GOD] ARE THEY WHO DID NOT SEE [ME] AND YET BELIEVED [IN ME]." (John 20:29 AMP)

Yes, we walk by faith. We love to sing, preach, dance, have special services called revivals, and testify about the goodness of the Lord. We, many times, view these services as evangelistic. Never forget, evangelism is taking the Word of God to the streets to convince fallen humanity of the love our heavenly Father have for them. Services inside the four-walled structure is mainly for believers although those without the love of Christ applied to their lives may enter as well and be blessed. Therefore, as we extrapolate Matthew 28:19, we have been given three methodologies for taking this gospel of Christ to the streets. The first command is "GO." The second is "TEACH." And the third is "BAPTIZE."

LET US TAKE A CLOSER LOOK AT MATTHEW 28:19:

1. "*Go*"—This means to ambulate, to move, to depart from one place to another, regardless of gender, ethnicity, religion, social or economic status. All who follow Jesus are commanded and commissioned to go into familiar and unfamiliar places to herald the fact that salvation comes through the shed blood of Jesus Christ.

   THEN THE MASTER TOLD THE SERVANT, GO OUT INTO THE HIGHWAYS AND ALONG THE HEDGES, AND COMPEL THEM TO COME IN, SO THAT MY HOUSE MAY BE FILLED [WITH GUESTS]. (Luke 14:23 AMP)

This text, as recorded by Luke, is an invitation rejected and filled with excuses, and now that invitation is extended to the poor.

THE SPIRIT OF THE LORD IS UPON ME [THE MESSIAH], BECAUSE HE HAS ANOINTED ME TO PREACH THE GOOD NEWS TO THE POOR. HE HAS SENT ME TO ANNOUNCE RELEASE [PARDON, FORGIVENESS] TO THE CAPTIVES, AND RECOVERY OF SIGHT TO THE BLIND, TO SET FREE THOSE WHO ARE OPPRESSED [DOWNTRODDEN, BRUISED, CRUSHED BY TRAGEDY]... TO PROCLAIM THE FAVORABLE YEAR OF THE LORD [THE DAY OF SALVATION AND THE FAVOR OF GOD ABOUND GREATLY]. (Luke 4:18–19 AMP)

The poor will now become the recipients of that which was designated for those who chose not to come to the celebration. Salvation is for all who accept Christ as their Lord and Savior. TIME IS SHORT. GO AND EVANGELIZE NOW. Without a doubt, we who accept this invitation to go will be rewarded with souls being added to the kingdom of God.

2. "*TEACH*"—One of the most difficult professions to be a part of is that of an educator. The difficulty of this profession is that learning and doing things differently than you are familiar with causes one to walk away from knowledge they are unacquainted with. The teacher is responsible to instruct, show, and explain to others the benefits of that which they are unaware of and what they desire to learn and appropriate into their lifestyles. Important for us to know is to have access to education which will empower us to do great exploits in the work of enlarging the kingdom of God. Systematic instructions should be a requirement for all phases of ministry.

NOT MANY [OF YOU] SHOULD BECOME TEACHERS [SERVING IN AN OFFICIAL TEACHING CAPACITY], MY BROTHERS AND SISTERS, FOR YOU KNOW THAT

WE [WHO ARE TEACHERS] WILL BE JUDGED BY A HIGHER STANDARD [BECAUSE WE HAVE ASSUMED GREATER ACCOUNTABILITY AND MORE CONDEMNATION IF WE TEACH INCORRECTLY]. (James 3:1 AMP)

An important lesson to learn from this verse is that teachers are held to a higher degree of accountability. Teaching builds and establishes foundational truth for us to live by while establishing and solidifying our faith. Therefore, 1 Timothy 4:8 (AMP) states, "FOR PHYSICAL TRAINING IS OF SOME VALUE, BUT GODLINESS [SPIRITUAL TRAINING] IS OF VALUE IN EVERYTHING AND IN EVERY WAY, SINCE IT HOLDS PROMISE FOR THE PRESENT LIFE AND FOR THE LIFE TO COME." Yes, teaching is empowering.

3. "*BAPTIZING*"—This is becoming immersed in that which has captured your attention. It is the initiation and submission of all of yourself to the ways of the thing or the one you desire to emulate. Romans 1:16 (NLT) epitomizes the commitment of one who identifies with the total personage of Christ: "FOR I AM NOT ASHAMED OF THIS GOOD NEWS ABOUT CHRIST. IT IS THE POWER OF GOD AT WORK, SAVING EVERYONE WHO BELIEVES—THE JEW FIRST AND ALSO THE GENTILE." Appropriate at this time is to reference the Christian hymn, "I HAVE DECIDED TO FOLLOW JESUS, NO TURNING BACK, NO TURNING BACK." As reported by https://renewaljournal.com, "This hymn originated in India. The lyrics are based on the last words of a man in Garo, Assam." The ceremony of baptism is water that indicates a union and a new identity with Christ through His life, death, and resurrection. His resurrection is the pivotal event that we base our hope in life eternal.

Our mission is clear because of the various doubts, fears, uncertainties, pessimistic attitudes, and our faithlessness. The need for compelling others to believe becomes so important and paramount that failure to evangelize is not an option, for we are promised power and authority to proclaim this glorious gospel throughout the world. This power and authority were made available to all on the day of Pentecost when the Holy Spirit appeared to empower and infuse us with boldness to do this great work of evangelism.

When you have become thoroughly involved with the science and art evangelism, you are moved with love and compassion for fallen humanity to the point that adding to the kingdom of God and sharing this glorious gospel takes precedence over church work. Church work is okay; however, "the work of the church" is the realization and the expectation that after hearing God's Word, it will be realized in the lives of others. Now, men and women, boys and girls will cry out, "WHAT MUST I DO TO BE SAVED?" the lives of others. This is so quintessentially important that failure to do the work of the church will result in a life-and-death struggle that will turn humanity not only against but to the rejection of the God of the Bible.

TO BE PERFECTLY CLEAR, THE RAPID NEED FOR RAPID DEPLOYMENT IS NOW.

CHAPTER 2

WAR, NO ESCAPE, PREREQUISITES FOR WINNING

FOR THOUGH WE WALK IN THE FLESH [AS MORTAL MEN], WE ARE
NOT CARRYING ON OUR [SPIRITUAL] WARFARE ACCORDING TO THE
FLESH AND USING THE WEAPONS OF MEN... THE WEAPONS OF OUR
WARFARE ARE NOT PHYSICAL [WEAPONS OF FLESH AND BLOOD].
OUR WEAPONS ARE DIVINELY POWERFUL FOR THE DESTRUCTION OF
FORTRESSES... WE ARE DESTROYING SOPHISTICATED ARGUMENTS AND
EVERY EXALTED AND PROUD THING THAT SETS ITSELF UP AGAINST
THE [TRUE] KNOWLEDGE OF GOD, AND WE ARE TAKING EVERY
THOUGHT AND PURPOSE CAPTIVE TO THE OBEDIENCE OF CHRIST.
—2 Corinthians 10:3–5 (AMP)

WAR

Based on our scriptural reference, from the day we accept Jesus
Christ as our Lord and Savior, our decision is now our introduction
to engage in a battle for our lives. Knowing that he is losing or have
lost you, Satan shifts to an offensive mode and will do whatever he
can to win you back or to destroy you. You are now his target for
destruction. When the enemy attacks, you must now fight the fight
of your life. Never forget, you cannot fight this battle on a physical
plain. Humanism, your networking skills, and your ability to joust

are not enough to fight this spiritual battle. Second Corinthians 10:4 (NLT) says, "WE USE GOD'S MIGHTY WEAPONS, NOT WORLDLY WEAPONS, TO KNOCK DOWN THE STRONGHOLDS OF HUMAN REASONING AND TO DESTROY FALSE ARGUMENTS."

We are at war. Now reconnaissance becomes necessary.

Reconnaissance is a mission to scout out or spy on our enemy to gain information on their activities and capabilities in battle. Knowing as much as you can about the enemy gives you an advantage for winning against such a formidable foe. First Peter 5:8 (AMP) says, "BE SOBER [WELL BALANCED AND SELF-DISCIPLINED], BE ALERT AND CAUTIOUS AT ALL TIMES. THAT ENEMY OF YOURS, THE DEVIL, PROWLS AROUND LIKE A ROARING LION [FIERCELY HUNGRY], SEEKING SOMEONE TO DEVOUR." This is war and the enemy wants to gulp you down. Be watchful.

There is an armed conflict going on around us, and for some of us, the collateral damage is doing more harm than the actual battle itself. The objective of this conflict is to distract and destroy. Thus, the collateral damage is the negative influence of those fighting to gain support for their individual concerns, which in turn will cause one to do some critical thinking and make the best decisions for their personal survival. When we make decisions and choices, we sometimes agree or disagree with the status quo, and our success in life may be compromised. We can call this collateral damage. The results of collateral damage are the severe consequences that an unintended target must suffer. Although the unintended target suffers severely, there can also be unintended consequences for a legitimate target. From the day an individual accepts the Lord Jesus Christ as their Savior, that person becomes a major target of the enemy of our lives, Satan. That decision to follow Christ is the introduction to engage in the battle for their lives. When the enemy knows that he is losing you, you now become his target for destruction. Collateral damage does not care who get hurt in the fight for your life. Whoever gets in his path, relentlessly, Satan goes into such a destructive mode that he will attack first the most vulnerable person he can influence. Hopefully, we are not in the wrong place at the wrong time. This kind of fighting can bring victory for some while harming the unsuspected and the innocent. Our question is "Who's on the Lord's side?"

The aim of this conflict is to destroy one's faith and confidence in God. Our faith is the substructure that you cannot see, yet it allows us to remain focused and determined. It motivates, strengthens, and encourages us with foundational trues that ensures us that the battle is already won. YES, WE ARE AT WAR.

John MacArthur stated in his book *The Truth War*, "WAR IS ONE OF THE MOST CALAMITOUS, CONSEQUENCES OF EVIL. IT IS CATASTROPHIC. IT IS ALWAYS UGLY. IT SHOULD NEVER BE GLAMORIZED, AND NO SANE PERSON SHOULD EVER DESIRE THE CONFLICT OR SAVOR THE STRIPE OF WAR."

Physical responses to spiritual battles are always insufficient and ineffective. MacArthur also said, "WHAT WE BELIEVE RATHER THAN WHAT WE DO IS WHAT SECURES US A RIGHTEOUS STANDING BEFORE GOD." Through the storms of life, I will continue to put my trust in the hand of our Lord and Savior Jesus Christ.

This war can bring persecutions, disappointed dreams and hopes, headaches, heartaches, bereavement, poverty, unemployment, systemic racism, police brutality, etc. John 10:10 (AMP) says, "THE THIEF COMES ONLY IN ORDER TO STEAL AND KILL AND DESTROY. I CAME THAT THEY HAVE AND ENJOY LIFE, AND HAVE IT IN ABUNDANCE [TO THE FULL, TILL IT OVERFLOW]." Because the thief has won many engagements, in his cockiness, he overlooks the eschatological outcome of the battle for those who is on the Lord's side—life and that more abundant. "WE WIN."

LET US LOOK AT THE THREE WEAPONS THE ENEMY WILL USE AGAINST US:

1. *STEAL*—This strategy is to affect your life in such a way that you will develop amnesia as to who you really are. Amnesia can be temporary; however, if you lose your self-esteem, the enemy can make your life so miserable that you will not be able to recognize yourself, and your faith in God will suffer greatly.

2. *KILL*—When we think of death, automatically, we assume cessation of life to our physical bodies. Death for a believer can be threefold: spiritual, physical, and eternal. This death or killing is spiritual. You suffer, your reputation is completely ruined, your existence becomes hopeless, and there seems to be no way of escape.

3. *DESTROY*—Satan wants to annihilate you. He desires to make your life hopeless and unforgiving. His desire is to destroy relationships, erase any knowledge of the reality of God in your life while attempting to get you to accept all alternative solutions to God's design for your life. This is a clear resolve in trusting in humanism over the Word of God. Never forget, without God, we are nothing.

This war from the believer's perspective is to fight and to protect all that they have been made steward over. Once faith has been established, it does not matter what type of conflict we are engaged in, nor does it matter the duration of the battle. We are assured that the battle is not ours but the Lord's. Second Chronicles 20:15c (AMP) states, "BE NOT AFRAID OR DISMAYED AT THIS GREAT MULTITUDE, FOR THE BATTLE IS NOT YOURS, BUT GOD'S." Faith is our confirmation that activates an inner source within us that augments and shapes our thought life to trust and know that our battles has been won more than two thousand years ago on the cross of calvary. Parenthetically, let me take a moment to say, "LOOK OUT, DEVIL, I'M ON THE LORD'S SIDE AND HIS SIDE IS THE WINNING SIDE." Okay, back to the war. To fight this war, we must stay in the Word of God.

NO ESCAPE

> HOW SHALL WE ESCAPE IF WE NEGLECT SO GREAT
> A SALVATION WHICH AT FIRST BEGAN TO BE SPO-
> KEN BY THE LORD AND WAS CONFIRMED UNTO US
> BY THEM THAT HEARD HIM. (Hebrews 2:3 KJV)

THERE IS NO WAY OUT, THERE IS NO ROUTE YOU CAN TAKE TO BYPASS THE NECESSARY PROCESS YOU NEED TO TAKE TO AVOID NEGATIVE OUTCOMES; UNLESS YOU ADHERE TO THE PROCLAMATION OF THE LORD, AND OF THOSE HE APPOINTED TO SHARE HIS GLORIOUS GOSPEL. AS A CONSEQUENCE OF NOT BELIEVING AND FOLLOWING THE WORDS OF THE LORD, THEN GLOOM AND DOOM IS YOUR FATE, AND THERE IS NO POSSIBLE WAY OF ESCAPE FROM THE ISSUES THAT ARE PERPLEXING YOU. (Hebrews 2:3 JRD/LSD)

Because of our commitment to Christ, Satan wants us to response to crisis in a manner that is out of character for a child of God. Therefore, Satan's attacks has and do come in ways that are unexpected. Yes, sometimes we are caught off guard and surprised at these unexpected situations. Matthew 7:15 (AMP) states, "BEWARE OF FALSE PROPHETS, (TEACHERS) WHO COME TO YOU DRESSED AS SHEEP [APPEARING GENTLE AND INNOCENT], BUT INWARDLY ARE RAVENOUS WOLVES."

Know this: any physical response to spiritual warfare is always insufficient and ineffective. So when the enemy comes against you with all his threats, know that God is greater than any opposition that will confront you. There is no escape without this knowledge.

BE SOBER [WELL BALANCED AND SELF-DISCIPLINED], BE ALERT AND CAUTIOUS AT ALL TIMES. THAT ENEMY OF YOURS, THE DEVIL, PROWLS AROUND LIKE A ROARING LION [FIERCELY HUNGRY] SEEKING SOMEONE TO DEVOUR. (1 Peter 5:8 AMP)

Our battle is a battle of and in the mind. There are instances when the enemy makes you think that this battle is all about you as he attacks you in a personal way, but I am here to tell you, nothing is about you; it is Satan's attempt to rid you of your God consciousness. This is not a war of flesh and blood; it is a war that attacks you in your faith walk with the Lord. If the enemy can shatter your faith, he is on the verge of fulfilling his purpose to steal, to kill, and to destroy. This is war, and do not forget, you are on the winning side. Whenever this roaring lion selects you as his target, there is hope and a foundational truth that is God for us is more than this world against us. HALLELUJAH! However, there is no escape without the knowledge of the Word of God. God first, and everything else second.

Dependence on self-effort, our humanism, our ability to barter, and using our networking skills to bring resolution to difficult situations and challenges will soon evaporate into the arena of unanswered prayers. We will quickly discover that the choices and decisions without divine intervention and divine permission only leads to a hopeless existence: BATTLE LOST.

No escape is doomed from start to finish. It is where we see no remedy and no positive outcome of our dilemma. Myles Munroe stated, "THE DEEPEST CRAVING OF THE HUMAN SPIRIT IS TO FIND A SENSE OF SIGNIFICANCE AND RELEVANCE. THE SEARCH FOR RELEVANCE IN LIFE IS THE ULTIMATE PURSUIT OF MAN—THE GREATEST TRAGEDY IN LIFE IS NOT DEATH, BUT LIFE WITHOUT A REASON. IT IS DANGEROUS TO BE ALIVE AND NOT KNOW WHY YOU WERE GIVEN LIFE."

I would like to add my opinion to what Dr. Munroe stated. "It is dangerous to be alive and think you know what you do not know. When you opt for me, myself, and I, you are doomed for failure. Remember and never forget, you are not alone in this world. You need me and I need you; otherwise, there is no escape from failure when you think everything is about you. This is simply saying, we need somebody to help us as we search for answers to difficult situations."

The cravings, the wants, and desires of the human spirit sometimes bypass common sense; therefore, failure is a given without any possibility of escape from life's vicissitudes. The place where we are currently, without dealing with any kinds of solutions, is the proverbial Groundhog Day. This day is when several events, good, bad, or indifferent are recurring in monotonous ways. That is, things are happening repeatedly in the exact same way. Ecclesiastes 1:9 (KJV) states, "THE THING THAT HATH BEEN, IT IS THAT WHICH SHALL BE, AND THAT WHICH IS DONE IS THAT WHICH SHALL BE DONE: AND THERE IS NO NEW THING UNDER THE SUN."

This verse in Ecclesiastes 1:9 is not referring to new endeavors that will benefit mankind but rather that the same pursuits to achieve a desired end remain the same as it was in the initial effort of finding resolution to a given situation.

We are in a place, from the Hebrew, that I will call *Tohu va-Bohu*. This is a place where we need to be rescued or we will sink in the quagmires of life's journey with no motivation, no enthusiasm, and no hope. This place in life is a place that is void, dark, and empty. This place emerged when Lucifer, the archangel, tried to usurp the authority of God our Creator. His pride caused all of creation to undergo a catastrophic shaking that resulted in the devastation of the utopia designed for mankind by God (Ezekiel 28:11–19, Isaiah 14:12–17). Thus, Genesis 1:2a (KJV) now states, "AND THE EARTH WAS WITHOUT FORM AND VOID; AND DARKNESS WAS UPON THE FACE OF THE DEEP."

The pride of Lucifer caused this horrific condition known as SIN. Sin is the innate quality within man to do wrong. It is not sinful acts that are considered sin although they are the consequence of sin, but rather, sin is found in our unregenerate nature. Without question, it is sin that has disrupted the perfect continuity of God's creation.

No escape is in juxtaposition with EVER LEARNING. Second Timothy 3:7 (KJV) states, "EVER LEARNING, AND NEVER ABLE TO COME TO THE KNOWLEDGE OF THE TRUTH." Ever learning is about one who has mastered various fields of endeavors without considering nor prioritizing what is most important and useful for their individual lives. Always wanting to acquire and have knowledge of something, without purpose, causes one's understanding to become atrophied.

Buddy Greene and Jeff Taylor wrote a song called "Denomination Blues," and the last stanza stated these words: "YOU CAN GO TO COLLEGE, YOU CAN GO TO SCHOOL, BUT IF YOU HAVEN'T GOT JESUS, YOU'RE NOTHING BUT AN EDUCATED FOOL AND THAT'S ALL." The lyrics of this song is clearly the best definition of ever learning and no escape I have ever heard. I have knowledge, and I am doing absolutely nothing with it. Ever learning—no escape.

The BibleRef.com interprets 2 Timothy 3:7 as "THOSE WHO ARE ALWAYS SEEKING THE NEWEST, LATEST, GREATEST SPIRITUAL TEACHING. IN MODERN TIMES, THIS IS SOMETIMES REFERRED TO AS A PERSON WHO IS SO OPEN-MINDED THAT THEIR BRAINS HAVE FALLEN OUT." Yes, ever learning—no escape. This attitude also reveals to us someone with all their learning that is trapped in yesterday's experiences and refuses to move from their comfort zone because of fear of the challenges they must face. Therefore, they are satisfied with what was and are never inspired nor motivated to tackle the present nor the future. Ever learning, trapped, no escape.

Ecclesiastes 1:4 (AMP) says, "I HAVE SEEN ALL THE WORKS WHICH HAVE BEEN DONE UNDER THE SUN, AND BEHOLD, ALL IS VANITY, A FUTILE GRASPING AND CHASING AFTER THE WIND." This verse teaches that repetition of the same old things day in and day out will make one's existence dull and uninteresting. No escape.

Crucial to everyone who wish to be successful in life is having a positive self-image. Being comfortable with who you are is vital for moving up the ladder of success. Never look down on others as if they are beneath you. It does not mean that you flaunt your God-given talent to make others feel less than you. There is no escape if we allow our talent to take us to a place where your character cannot keep us.

All of us are special and unique because we have been individualized by God. Therefore, we must see ourselves as God sees us. In each of us is a treasure. We must be careful because Satan desires to sift us as wheat. His goal is to humiliate, annihilate, and to give us enough rope so that we hang ourselves. Charles Capps stated of one's self-image, "HIS IMAGE OF HIMSELF CAN CARRY HIM TO HEIGHTS OF

SUCCESS OR PLUNGE HIM TO DEPTHS OF DEFEAT AND DESPAIR." Keep your eyes on Jesus because without Him, there is no escape.

PREREQUISITE FOR WINNING

> LET IT BE KNOWN AND CLEARLY UNDERSTOOD BY ALL OF YOU, AND BY ALL THE PEOPLE OF ISRAEL, THAT IN THE NAME OF JESUS THE NAZARENE, WHOM YOU [DEMANDED BE] CRUCIFIED [BY THE ROMANS AND], WHOM GOD RAISED FROM THE DEAD—IN THE NAME [THAT IS, BY THE AUTHORITY AND POWER OF JESUS] THIS MAN STANDS HERE BEFORE YOU IN GOOD HEALTH… THIS JESUS IS THE STONE WHICH WAS DESPISED AND REJECTED BY YOU, THE BUILDERS, BUT WHICH BECAME THE CHIEF CORNERSTONE… AND THERE IS SALVATION IN NO ONE ELSE; FOR THERE IS NO OTHER NAME UNDER HEAVEN THAT HAS BEEN GIVEN AMONG PEOPLE BY WHICH WE MUST BE SAVED [FOR GOD HAS PROVIDED THE WORLD NO ALTERNATIVE FOR SALVATION]. (Acts 4:10–12 AMP)

Onomastics or onomatology is the history, origin, and study of the use of proper names. It is also referred to as the science of naming. A name is a label or an identifier that distinguishes an individual or something from another person or something else. Without seeing, you may vocalize one's name, and the expectation is that an immediate response will follow from the one whom you are addressing.

> A GOOD NAME IS RATHER TO BE CHOSEN THAN GREAT RICHES, AND LOVING FAVOR RATHER THAN SILVER AND GOLD. (Proverbs 22:1 KJV)

This verse in Proverbs 22:1 says that a name is generally expected to reflect who you are, which reflects your character and personality.

Most importantly, your character and personality states that you cannot be bought or bribed. A name may gather significance based on the importance we apply to it; otherwise, there is no psychological significance to it. Thank God for a good name.

The first names were derived from flowers (*rose, violet, daisy*), months (*April, May, June*), precious stones (*ruby, pearl*) and places (*Georgia, Dakota*).

Now, surnames were based on one's occupation (*Hunter, Barber, Forest, Fisher*) or their place of origin (*Paul of Tarsus, Jesus of Nazareth*).

Some names of persons were and are difficult to spell or pronounce, so we opted for what we call nicknames to substitute for their proper names. And in most cases, you never know the proper name of an individual until we attend their homegoing service.

The necessity for dealing with a name is based on the prerequisite for winning. The names used for God emphasizes His character, personality, His ability to meet our needs, and His authority.

The Bible clearly teaches that the only name that brings salvation to fallen humanity is the name of Jesus. Learning the proper use of the name of Jesus opens the doors of unlimited possibilities. Now, this word, *prerequisite*, indicates that for the usage of the name of Jesus to be effective, you MUST know something about His name before attempting to use it. With knowledge and understanding as to who Jesus is, and great expectations as to the outcome of your prayer requests, you will quickly discover that prayer, coupled with faith, brings into reality that which you at one time thought was impossible. However, unless you are intimately involved with Him, surface knowledge will be ineffective when it comes to answered prayers. The more you know about Jesus should create an appetite and a thirst for His Word. Faith moves God on your behalf.

Let us look at what God says concerning the mistreatment of His people, which will give us a better knowledge of who He is. This mistreatment gives rise to the prerequisite for winning and the need for rapid deployment. We can see in our society today that the reality of God should be based on His Word; however, that reality is instead based on those who represent and claim to have a personal relationship with Him. Sadly, and to our dismay, the old cliché exposes the impostors. It states, "YOU NEED TO WALK THE WALK INSTEAD OF TALKING THE TALK." Some of those who claim to know Christ are not good examples of the One whom they represent. There is another cliché according to your faith that is embraced: "DO AS I SAY, NOT AS I DO." The prerequisite for winning is denying our personal agendas and following the Word of God whatever the cost. There is a question you as a believer must face: Have you really decided to follow Jesus in the light of all distractions?

In several situations, we attach ourselves to leadership or to those whom we think knows more than we know, and rather than searching the Scriptures, we tend to accept the words of the ones we trust. Salvation is not based on individuals but on Jesus the Christ. Ezekiel 34:1–10 talks about the shepherds whose greed and corruption polluted the people of God and their failed leadership that exploited God's people. Verses 11–31 of this same chapter, God warns the shepherds of their nefarious actions, that He will bring restoration to His people who had been scattered. We must remember, nothing is about us; it is all about our Lord and Savior. The prerequisite for winning is Jesus first.

Winning is gaining victory in all you do. The reason for this statement is that in every aspect of life, you are always a winner because you learn from every experience. Upward mobility in life is always based on how you think and navigate your journey in life. Therefore, when you attach the word *prerequisite* to winning, with the understanding that knowledge of Jesus is key critical to your success, then you can declare with certainty you are a winner in all that you attempt to do.

Philippians 4:13 (KJV) says, "I CAN DO ALL THINGS THROUGH CHRIST WHICH STRENGTHENETH ME." So then, the winning formula is simple: submission to the will and way of Jesus is a guarantee for success. There is something about the name Jesus that when invoked, demons tremble, healing eclipses sickness, and diseases, serendipitously, ways and means for existence, are already worked out. The seed for winning is so small that we cannot imagine the potential it will yield. Sometimes, we try to rush the process, but let me remind you, maturation takes time. Therefore, do not compare yourself to anyone but the King of kings and the Lord of lords. Likewise, for you to be a winner, you need to go through the process of learning and putting learned information into practical application. God's timing is more important than our timing.

Winning souls to the kingdom of God is not about your individual skills; it is about what is in you that you can share with someone else who then will alter their lifestyles according to what they embrace.

The prerequisite of winning is your due diligence to any field of endeavor you apply yourself to. Jesus is the reason for our existence, and He is exactly what we need to be winners. The Scriptures employ us to study and hide the Word of God within us. With this as our guide, we can only excel in our efforts to increase the kingdom of God.

CHAPTER 3

THE ENEMY THAT BLOCKS OUR PATH

BE SOBER [WELL BALANCED AND SELF-DISCIPLINED],
BE ALERT AND CAUTIOUS AT ALL TIMES. THAT ENEMY OF
YOURS, THE DEVIL, PROWLS AROUND LIKE A ROARING LION
[FIERCELY HUNGRY], SEEKING SOMEONE TO DEVOUR.
—1 Peter 5:8 (AMP)

One of the key things to be cognizant of when applying for employment is to have as much knowledge of the company or organization you desire to work for. Knowing their history, their status, their projections, their strengths and weaknesses, and any other pertinent information pertaining to their company is paramount.

The goal of every believer is to build and expand the kingdom of God on earth. For every good work you attempt to do, always have knowledge of the opposition to your efforts. There is always an enemy that will block your path; that is, to block your effort in completing your assignment for kingdom building. An enemy is anyone who cherishes resentment or malicious purpose toward another. This enemy is not your friend; he is very deceptive, he is your adversary, your foe, whose main objective is to bring unrest to your efforts of kingdom building.

The prowess of this tactician has always been referred to Satan or the thief as recorded in John 10:10a (KJV), "THE THIEF COMETH NOT, BUT TO STEAL, AND TO KILL, AND TO DESTROY." This is a natural expectation of the enemy because Satan's goal is our complete destruction. More so, his efforts are to topple the kingdom of his Creator.

The enemy I am speaking of here is not a family member, not your neighbor, not the person that does not like you, and it is not Satan although he is a vile and vicious opponent of righteousness. This enemy I am speaking of here is "SELF." Self is an individual known or considered as the subject of his own consciousness. Proverbs 23:7a (AMP) says, "FOR AS HE THINKS IN HIS HEART, SO IS HE [IN BEHAVIOR—ONE WHO MANIPULATES]." Also, let us see what Psalm 12:1–2 (AMP) says, in my translation of self, "SAVE AND HELP AND RESCUE, LORD FOR GODLY PEOPLE CEASE TO BE. FOR THE FAITHFUL VANISH FROM AMONG THE SONS OF MEN... THEY SPEAK DECEITFUL AND WORTHLESS WORDS TO ONE ANOTHER; WITH FLATTERING LIPS AND A DOUBLE HEART THEY SPEAK."

Self, according to Vocabulary.com, comes from the Old English, in which it means "one's own person." Self is anyone who is considered having a distinct personality. That speak of having character, choice, and integrity which constitutes and characterizes and distinguishes one as a person. Character consists of the ethical, mental, and principles of right and wrong behavior that distinguishes us as an individual. Therefore, I am who I am by what I embrace.

As the creative expression of God, man was placed into a perfect environment with a predisposition to think and choose his path after receiving instructions as to what is expected of him in the environment created by the words of God. The validation of this relationship with the Creator was based on man's free will to fellowship with God or not.

Having a choice entails preference, election, the authority, and privilege of choosing. Self indicates that we are free moral agents with the ability to accept or reject an edict that has been given. Of course, God could have erased choice from who we are; if so, we would be no more than and no less than a robot. Choice distinguishes us from all other creative acts of God and makes us special. When God created man, He said of him that he was (in my own words) incredibly good. Since we have made a choice as to our deportment, then the consequences of our thought process have crystalized into the kind of person, the kind of people, the kind of society we are today. The negative influences that we have embraced now defines self as a product of all that we have decided that is relevant for our existence.

With clarity of thought, we can and should pursue the goals we have set for ourselves. The issue that we face is found in Galatians 6:4–5 (AMP): "BUT EACH ONE MUST CAREFULLY SCRUTINIZE HIS OWN WORK [EXAMINING HIS ACTIONS, ATTITUDES, AND BEHAVIOR], AND THEN HE CAN HAVE THE PERSONAL SATISFACTION AND INNER JOY OF DOING SOMETHING COMMENDABLE WITHOUT COMPARING HIMSELF TO ANOTHER... FOR EVERY PERSON WILL HAVE TO BEAR [WITH PATIENCE] HIS OWN BURDEN [OF FAULTS AND SHORTCOMINGS FOR WHICH ALONE IS RESPONSIBLE]."

You must, without question, learn to take charge of you, yourself, because it is only you that can take you to where you want to go. Always remember, without God, you are a failure before you start. Take charge of you. You are your worst enemy, and you are or will be trapped in this existence unless you recognize God as sovereign over all. The enemy that blocks your path is "YOU."

Time is out for the blame game. Take charge of you, pull yourself together, and move forward and excel in every endeavor you attempt. All the negative things you can imagine with their individual consequences, God sees and knows every trial, every test, every challenge you are facing. This is where your faith kicks in and take you beyond the present circumstances so that you can envision and see what God has already accomplished for you. Take charge of you. As the apostle Paul stated in 2 Corinthians 9:27 (AMP), "BUT [LIKE A BOXER] I STRICTLY DISCIPLINE MY BODY AND MAKE IT MY SLAVE, SO THAT, AFTER I HAVE PREACHED [THE GOSPEL] TO OTHERS, I MYSELF WILL NOT SOMEHOW BE DISQUALIFIED [AS UNFIT FOR SERVICE]."

You are only one moment, one decision away from your escape, from your deliverance; therefore, take charge of you. There is nothing good in self, but you have the power and authority to corral this enemy that is blocking your path of deliverance, hope, peace, and success. Take charge of you. The wrestling with self causes one's human nature and the propensity to sin to become more prevalent. But with God, the enemy that blocks your path can be brought under subjection. The struggle with self may seem long, hard, and exceedingly difficult, to the point of wanting to give up because the struggle with me, myself, and I seems to be a never-ending saga. Let me encourage you, with God you have the victory; you are a winner. Take charge of you. The enemy that blocks your path is a defeated foe. Girt yourself with the armor of God and walk in His strength. You can keep your body under subjection. This means that you have temperance, as recorded in Galatians 5:23, which is self-control.

Remember, self is who you are, your identity. Those whom you are unfamiliar with will never know the real you. With those you are close to, you are transparent, or should I say, you are an open book. Therefore, you in all situations must unequivocally take charge of self. Human wisdom is reliance upon self as a solution, and in many cases, human wisdom goes opposite to God's Word.

CHAPTER 4

TRAINING AND EQUIPMENT

ALSO, I HEARD THE VOICE OF THE LORD SAYING, WHOM SHALL I
SEND, AND WHO WILL GO FOR US? THEN I SAID, HERE AM I; SEND ME.
—Isaiah 6:8 (KJV)

TRAINING

First things first, we need training in evangelism before we can effectively use the equipment (which is permanent, tried, and fixed) for presenting Jesus Christ to a lost world.

If you were asked, how do you know God exists or is the Creative Being you have determined is God is real or just an illusion? Our response is key critical in decision-making for those who need help believing that the God of the Bible exists. First Peter 3:15 (AMP) states, "BUT IN YOUR HEARTS SET CHRIST APART [AS HOLY—ACKNOWLEDGING HIM, GIVING FIRST PLACE IN YOUR LIVES] AS LORD. ALWAYS BE READY TO GIVE A [LOGICAL] DEFENSE TO ANYONE WHO ASKS YOU TO ACCOUNT FOR THE HOPE AND CONFIDENT ASSURANCE [ELICITED BY FAITH] THAT IS WITHIN YOU, YET [DO IT] WITH GENTLENESS AND RESPECT."

Therefore, training is of the utmost importance because you, number one, must have a personal encounter with the One whom you have pledged your fidelity. Before you can convince others about the love of God, you must be a partaker of that love. Darrell W.

Robinson stated in his book *People Sharing Jesus*, "CHRISTIAN WIT-NESSING IS NOT ABOUT ATTEMPTING TO FORCE IDEOLOGIES AND IDEAS ON OTHERS. IT IS ABOUT CARING PEOPLE WHO HAVE EXPERIENCED GOD'S LOVE AND GRACE CARRYING OUT THE ASSIGNMENT OF THE ALMIGHTY GOD TO SHARE HIS MESSAGE WITH OTHERS." Knowing God in this manner will cancel any doubts that one may have. That experience, regardless to opposition, cannot be denied. Never forget, no one knows your personal experience but you; therefore, you cannot make me doubt this truth of change, motivation, and excitement for sharing the love and grace of God for His people. The salvific process is proof that the God of the Bible completed a work in you that no other entity on the face of this earth could do.

At some point in your past, you were a liar, a thief, a hypocrite, a cheat—you name it, we have all been there. But through the shed blood of Jesus Christ, I, you, and all who have experienced the salvation of Christ have been and is changed. Second Corinthians 5:17 (AMP) states, "THEREFORE IF ANYONE IS IN CHRIST [THAT IS, GRAFTED IN, JOINED TO HIM BY FAITH IN HIM AS SAVIOR], HE IS A NEW CREATURE [REBORN AND RENEWED BY THE HOLY SPIRIT]; THE OLD THINGS [THE PREVIOUS MORAL AND SPIRITUAL CONDITION] HAVE PASSED AWAY. BEHOLD, NEW THINGS HAVE COME [BECAUSE SPIRITUAL AWAKENING BRINGS A NEW LIFE]." So then, my training begins with getting to know the One who saved and rescued me from a dangerous existence to a radical new lifestyle that has changed my perspectives from gloom and doom to one that is filled with possibilities unlimited in Christ.

The enemy of our lives uses our past to intimidate, shame, and persecute us with the objective of stimming our growth and prosperity. Connecting with Christ and being in fellowship and agreement with Him is a guarantee of success holistically. Before I can help and teach others, I must do some introspection about my faith relationship with the God of the Bible.

The next step in our training is to become acquainted with the Word of God. Why? Jeremiah 1:12 (AMP) states, "THEN SAID THE

Lord to me, "You have seen well, for I am alert and [actively] watching over my word to perform it."

God does not respond to your talent, your networking skills, nor to your shouting and dancing (spiritual gymnastics) or your prayers, and certainly not to the multiplicity of words inculcated in your vocabulary. For Him to perform for you, He looks at the amount of His Word that is in you. The reason for this is bound in 2 Timothy 2:13 (AMP): "If we are faithless, he remains faithful [true to his word and his righteous character], for he cannot deny himself." Therefore, David stated of God in Psalm 119:11 (AMP): "Your word have I treasured and stored in my heart, that I may not sin against you."

Therefore, the less Word in you, the less He watches over you because there is little or no Word in you for Him to perform. Therefore, we must study His Word so that we can know Him in an intimate way. This is what training is all about if we expect to know Him in every possible way. Once you know, then you will realize that Satan can only steal the tangible things [your family, your job, your riches, your house, and such like things]. But he cannot steal the intangible [your wealth, your hope, your faith, your character, nor your integrity or your peace]. Therefore, get in the Word and stay there. In His Word, all your needs are manifested and brought into fruition.

Learn and know all you can about your Savior. Knowing Him is the key to open all doors of possibilities, and it will equip you to handle all issues pertaining to you and your ability to share the gospel of Christ. Darrell Robinson also stated, "Every Christian has been equipped to share about Jesus with the Word of God and a personal testimony of their own experience of salvation."

Equipment

After going through a life-changing experience and doing some introspection and discovering your strengths and weaknesses in knowing Jesus, it is now time to equip yourselves with protective gear so that sharing the message of Jesus Christ will have its desired effect. Yet there are those who will be unable to physically go into the cities, states, nations, and the world; however, this battle can be undergirded by intercessors and prayer warriors and supporters (spiritually or financially). By whatever means necessary, enlarging God's kingdom is a mandate we must fulfill.

Perry Stone stated in his book *There's a Crack in Your Armor* that he had observed four types of soldiers in the body of Christ: (1) those who know nothing about the armor of God, (2) those who know something about the armor of God but refuse to wear it, (3) the soldiers who pick and choose their protection, wearing some but not all the armor, and (4) those Christians who wear the entire armor of God and actually know what it represents and how to use it.

For one to be skilled in their craft, to avoid being collateral damage, you must learn all you can about the equipment to use in this battle for humanity and begin to test it before entering the battlefield with untested equipment. You can discover this armor [*loin girt about with truth, breastplate of righteousness, feet shod with the preparation of the gospel of peace, the shield of faith, the helmet of salvation, and the Sword of the Spirit*] in Perry Stones's book as well as Ephesians chapter 6. Once you have become acquainted with this equipment, it is now time to begin to test each piece. Each piece of this equipment or armor is effective, and you will need to enlist the assistance of a trusted and experienced instructor to guide you in the use of this armor in this battle for lost souls. This does not negate your proficiency in the understanding of God's Word, but rather, it is an acknowledgment that we need a unified effort to defeat our most formidable foe. We often misquote the Scriptures when it comes to this team effort.

The Bible asks a question in Deuteronomy 32:30a (AMP), and we changed the context of the text and make it a declarative statement. One can chase a thousand and two can put ten thousand to flight. The Scripture states, "*HOW* [the operative word] COULD ONE CHASE *A THOUSAND*, AND *TWO* PUT *TEN THOUSAND* TO FLIGHT" (emphasis mine). Being equipped and trained in the Word of God, Leviticus

26:7–8 (AMP) will give us the definition of you, me, and others operating as a team: "AND YOU WILL CHASE YOUR ENEMIES, AND THEY WILL FALL BEFORE YOU BY THE SWORD… *FIVE* OF YOU WILL CHASE *A HUNDRED*, AND *A HUNDRED* OF YOU WILL PUT *TEN THOUSAND* TO FLIGHT; AND YOUR ENEMIES WILL FALL BEFORE YOU BY THE SWORD" (emphasis mine). To defeat the enemy, we need to properly interpret the text. Everything you need is in the text. Get in the Word and stay there. Apart from the text, our existence becomes a great struggle.

Having the right equipment for warfare and knowledge of its effectiveness is a guaranteed victory. We need to know that evangelism is a *BOOTS ON THE GROUND* ministry.

The mission of evangelism is to proclaim Jesus Christ as the Savior of all humanity, and without Him, a deleterious and chaotic lifestyle will continue to be the center stage of our objective reality. An objective and productive life depends on being connected to the proper source. That source is found in John chapter 15. Also, John 16:13–14 assures us that we are not alone in our efforts to promote this gospel of Christ. The Holy Spirit is always there to lead and guide us.

Evangelism is a one-on-one ministry. However, the pastoral and professional approaches to evangelism are part of what I call the threefold aspect of evangelism (personal or one-on-one ministry reaching individuals for Christ and pastoral and professional) approaches which are very necessary for retention and continuous growth of those who have committed their lives to Christ and the continual building of His kingdom.

To avoid compromising your character, integrity, and bringing shame to this most necessary ministry in the body of Christ, we need to stay focused on the mission and calling we have been called to and to teach and preach Jesus Christ and Him only as the solution to the deprived condition and the only hope of this world. We need to make sure that our words and opinions are in alignment with God's Word.

Boots on the ground is a strategic ministry that should be well planned through reconnaissance, getting the proper data on the community you are going to share this gospel, and never forget, you are the example that this world needs. The data needed should include the demographics as to private housing, apartment dwellers, cultural and racial makeup of the targeted community, the size of the families (be it single or two-parent home, and the lifestyle choice in each). Our mission is not to be judgmental but rather to teach and preach Jesus Christ.

> FOR GOD DID NOT SEND THE SON INTO THE WORLD TO JUDGE AND CONDEMN THE WORLD [THAT IS, TO INITIATE THE FINAL JUDGMENT OF THE WORLD], BUT THAT THE WORLD MIGHT BE SAVED THROUGH HIM. (John 3:17 AMP)

When going into these communities, always travel in groups of two or more persons. Never travel alone. This will aid in avoiding controversy in the different demographics of the communities. Each group should consist of both male and female Christian workers, full of faith and conviction and a deep love for mankind. Make sure you carry your Bible, the Gospel of John, or the New Testament, not only in your hearts but in your hand. Have specific Scriptures *highlighted* concerning salvation (*the need*, Romans 3:23, 6:23; *the cost*, 1 Corinthians 15:3–4; *the way*, John 1:12; *the joy*, Acts 8:37–39; *the term*, Luke 14:26–33; *the act*, Revelation 3:20; and *the seal*, Ephesians 1:13–14). You will also need your identification badge, community church groups that are supporting your efforts, a scratch pad, pen and pencil, and a church bulletin and tracts if possible. THE NEED FOR RAPID DEPLOYMENT IS NOW.

Three things to be considered by every nonbeliever:

1. Realize that you are alienated from God by your life choices.
2. You must have a desire to quit all wrongdoing that prevent Christ from having a place of priority in your life.
3. Renounce choices and decisions that impeded your spiritual growth and accept Jesus as Lord and Savior.

There is a song that I feel will express the purpose, the aim, and the goal of evangelism in a meaningful way. For the past twenty-five to thirty years, this song has been a blessing to me and those who work in fellowship sharing the good news of Jesus Christ to our communities. The impact of this song has changed my perspective in presenting this gospel in the streets, prison, nursing homes, and churches. This song was placed on the internet on Sunday, April 24, 2011, as part of their inspirational articles and instructional videos by Literature Missionary Connection. This is song number 123 in "The Better Living Crusade" songbook, compiled by Ronald and Equila Wright:

Ringing Doorbells for My Lord
(*To the tune of "Leaning on the Everlasting Arms"*)

Getting' up out our pews, going two by two's,
Ringing Doorbells for my Lord,
Serving God and man,
Sharing God's great plan,
Ringing doorbells for my Lord. (Chorus)

Gathering into bands,
Traveling through the land,
Ringing doorbells for my Lord.
Everyone we'll tell,
Even those in jail,
Ringing doorbells for my Lord. (Chorus)

Oh, how sweet to walk,
Round and round the block,
Ringing doorbells for my Lord;
Wearing out my shoes,
Telling God's Good News;
Ringing doorbells for my Lord. (Chorus)

Chorus
Ringing, ringing, ringing doorbells for my Lord,
Ringing, ringing, ringing doorbells for my Lord.

CHAPTER 5

GET UP FROM SITTING DOWN—"BOOTS ON THE GROUND"

AND THE LORD SAID UNTO THE SERVANT, GO OUT
INTO THE HIGHWAYS AND HEDGES, AND COMPEL THEM
TO COME IN, THAT MY HOUSE MAY BE FILLED.
—Luke 14:23 (KJV)

LET US PRAY: "Father, thank You for this opportunity where we can come together to honor and adore You, and that our collective efforts and thoughts are to and for the betterment of our community cities, states, nation, and the world that have been assigned to our hands. Be with us now as we take Your glorious gospel to the streets. Dear God, give us the strength and the fortitude to perform at the highest level of our ability so that men and women, boys and girls will come into the knowledge of who You are, and that Your directives will become the chosen path that all of us will adhere to. I pray that Your divine will and presence will be with us and that souls will be added to Your kingdom.

"We pray that You give us what to say, how to say it, and when to say words that will strengthen, give hope and encouragement in a time of need, and to cause one to develop hope in seemingly hopeless situations, that their dreams will be realized, and most importantly, that Your name will be glorified and praised and honored. In Your name we pray. Amen."

We, the church of God, have been instructed by our Lord to take His invitation of inclusion to the street, neighborhood, and communities where we live, and to be so convincing that those that hear will freely receive this request and join in fellowship with Him as well as for dinner. The use of the word *dinner* is for all needs being supplied by Christ Jesus. In Matthew 11:28 (KJV), Jesus says, "COME UNTO ME, ALL YE THAT LABOUR AND ARE HEAVY LADEN, AND I WILL GIVE YOU REST." Rest is being relaxed and renewed in your physical and mental strength. When we rest in peace, this is total reliance on God who is our Peace Giver. When you are at peace in God, every situation with its degrees of ups and downs will never overwhelm you. You are safe in the arms of the Lord. Also, resting is trusting God through all circumstances with the greatest of confidence. With this same confidence, we can now take this understanding of rest to the streets. Boots on the ground.

Taking this message of faith, hope, and love to the streets or boots on the ground is one of the best methods to use in fighting this battle for lost humanity. I say lost humanity because when there is a disconnect from the source that emits life, death will soon follow. This death is first spiritual then physical and, finally, eternal. To avoid death in either of these forms, it is incumbent on the part of the church of God to take this gospel beyond the four-walled structure of the church building. The assurance we have is knowing that the Lord has promised to be with us in this most valiant effort. So then, we must be watchful of the enemy because distractions, discouragement, and self-reliance are his tools to destroy our faith. Being filled with the anointing presence of our Lord, we know that we are already winners through Him that loves us.

Remember, when you are approaching the enemy, remain focused with your eyes on Christ. What was the response of the twelve spies as they were on reconnaissance to spy out the land of Canaan as instructed by Moses? With a pessimistic view, they only saw gloom and doom. Amidst their search, they saw fortified cities, and the inhabitants were giants, which made them feel as if the battle was over before it begun. Also, in their eyes, their self-image made them feel that they looked like grasshoppers. Although promised by God that they would be victorious in this battle, fear gripped their hearts, and ten of the spies returned with a negative report emphasizing the difficulty of winning this battle.

Victory in any venue is only experienced because of faith in leadership and knowing that whatever God has said, it's done. Although ten spies responded to what they physically saw, however, two looked beyond their situation and understood that one with God is a majority. Luke 1:37 (KJV) says, "For with God nothing shall be impossible." Hindered by unbelief causes you to embrace the negative and accept it as truth. However, we are taught by the Scriptures, where there is two or three touching and agreeing, the Lord will be in the midst. Therefore, until you willingly and enthusiastically hold on to what you have heard as truth, upward mobility will always be impossible. If you allow your mind to breed on things uncharacteristic for a believer, boots on the ground will not have its desired effect. Therefore, we must remain focused and steadfast toward our objective.

It is now time for us to move from where we are to where we need to go. Boots on the ground will take us to higher heights and deeper depths in the work of evangelism. Let us get up from sitting down. Why? God cannot use us sitting down.

Successes and failures are based on how we maneuver through life based on the goals we have envisioned for ourselves. Achieving the planned objectives is motivation for future task. If I can change just one thing within my community that will have lasting effects or change the mindset of one individual that others view as impossible to change, then achieving this goal will instill a sense of accomplishment that brings to realization that had I not attempted to make a difference, an entire society of people could have possibly been lost and unproductive. Therefore, we need to take this gospel to the streets. Boots on the ground is necessary for the salvation of the world.

The plan is not complicated for one to receive the salvation of God, but rather, it is an amazingly simple exercise:

(1) Realize that you, through your own volition, have chosen a lifestyle that is antithetical to that of our Savior. This realization will cause one to realize that a life without Christ will lead to an existence directly opposed to that of our Lord. Thus, we are classified as sinners. Attesting to this, Luke 18:13–14 (The Book, Tyndale House Publishers, Inc.) says, "BUT THE CORRUPT TAX COLLECTOR STOOD AT A DISTANCE AND DARED NOT EVEN LIFT HIS EYES TO HEAVEN AS HE PRAYED, BUT BEAT UPON HIS CHEST IN SORROW, EXCLAIMING, GOD, BE MERCIFUL TO ME, A SINNER… I TELL YOU, THIS SINNER, NOT THE PHARISEE, RETURNED HOME FORGIVEN! FOR THE PROUD SHALL BE HUMBLED, BUT THE HUMBLE SHALL BE HONORED."

(2) Knowing that you are alien from the plan of salvation, ask for forgiveness and repent of everything that you are aware of that keeps you separated from Christ. Acts 3:19 (AMP) states, "SO REPENT [CHANGE YOUR INNER SELF—YOUR OLD WAY OF THINKING, REGRET PAST SINS] AND RETURN [TO GOD—SEEK HIS PURPOSE FOR YOUR LIFE], SO THAT YOUR SINS MAY BE WIPED AWAY [BLOTTED OUT, COMPLETELY ERASED], SO THAT TIMES OF REFRESHING MAY COME FROM THE PRESENCE OF THE LORD [RESTORING YOU LIKE A COOL WIND ON A HOT DAY]."

(3) Being consciously aware of your personal status before God, and you have asked for forgiveness for all wrongdoings, the next thing is to acknowledge Jesus as your Lord and Savior. John 1:12 (AMP) states, "BUT AS MANY AS DID RECEIVE AND WELCOME HIM, HE GAVE THE RIGHT [AUTHORITY, THE PRIVILEGE] TO BECOME CHILDREN OF GOD, THAT IS, TO THOSE WHO BELIEVE IN (ADHERE TO, TRUST IN, AND RELY ON) HIS NAME."

Boots on the ground is the catalyst for meeting those separated from God and having a dialogue to share the love story of Jesus Christ. Certainly, we may not win them all, but we will win some now and more later as the Word of God takes root in their hearts. Therefore, get on up from sitting down. God cannot use you sitting down.

The work in the church, in every department, should have as its aim the promotion of evangelism. This is where boots on the ground gets its start. The genesis of this ministry is to recognize that our goal in the church is winning souls into the kingdom of God. The key to evangelization is the layman. Therefore, we must build a program that will galvanize, motivate, recruit, and train the layman in this necessary ministry. Although lost humanity was scattered through-out the world, the apostles and the laymen were the instruments God used to carry His Word to His people. This is getting up from sitting down and boots on the ground in action.

When the work of evangelism is carried out properly, souls will be added daily to the church—that is, the body of Christ. By using the multiplication principle, for every soul you win, one more is added to the kingdom of God. You plus that one equals two. For every two you gain, that is you and the one you gained taking the Gospel message to the streets, you now gain four.

So then, every 4×4 is a gain of 16 and 16×16 equals 256, and so on. Since 99 percent of the church consist of laymen. If they fail to take this Gospel to the streets and are also *Absent Without Official Leave*, the effectiveness of evangelism will be in doubt.

After winning souls to Christ, they must be trained and equipped to evangelize. Ninety-five percent of all converts never win anyone to Christ because they are not trained nor equipped for this task. Rather than being excited as to how large your congregation is, it is obvious that training a person to evangelize effectively will be more fruitful. This is what I call doing the work of the church instead of church work. We need boots on the ground.

THE NEED FOR RAPID DEPLOYMENT IS NOW

THERE ARE THREE QUALIFICATIONS FOR THOSE WORKING IN THE FIELD:

(1) YOU MUST HAVE A CLEAR, VIVID CONCEPTION OF THE GOSPEL OF CHRIST.

> I AM NOT ASHAMED OF THE GOSPEL, FOR IT IS THE POWER OF GOD FOR SALVATION [FROM HIS WRATH AND PUNISHMENT] TO EVERYONE WHO BELIEVES [IN CHRIST AS SAVIOR], TO THE JEW FIRST AND ALSO TO THE GREEK. (Romans 1:16 AMP)

(2) YOU MUST HAVE A DEEP LOVE FOR LOST HUMANITY.

> OH, THAT MY EYES WERE A FOUNTAIN OF TEARS, I WOULD WEEP FOREVER; I WOULD SOB DAY AND NIGHT FOR THE SLAIN OF MY PEOPLE! (Jeremiah 9:1 The Book, Tyndale House Publishers, Inc.)

(3) YOU MUST HAVE A CAPACITY FOR LEADERSHIP. Dr. Myles Munroe stated in his book *The Spirit of Leadership*,

> GENUINE LEADERSHIP IS NOT A RESULT OF MEMORIZING FORMULAS, LEARNING SKILLS, IMITATING METHODS, OR TRAINING IN TECHNIQUES. IT IS AN ATTITUDE OF THE HEART… EVERY HUMAN HAS THE INSTINCT AND CAPACITY FOR LEADERSHIP, BUT MOST DO NOT HAVE THE COURAGE OR WILL TO CULTIVATE IT… THE NUMBER ONE NEED ALL OVER THE GLOBE TODAY IS NOT MONEY, SOCIAL PROGRAMS, OR EVEN NEW GOVERNMENTS, IT IS QUALITY, MORAL, DISCIPLINED, PRINCIPLE-CENTERED LEADERSHIP.

These qualifications are so desperately necessary that without them, reaching the lost will be stymied by our unpreparedness for the assigned task. All who name the name of the Lord as their personal Savior must be aware of the holiness of God, understand the transformative power of the cross, and know that, pertaining to humankind, all have sinned. This knowledge prepares you to move forward in the work of the Lord.

We who claim salvation should never be judgmental of other. The love of God eradicates the sin element in all who repents. This same love must be exemplified in the lives of believers toward others through the winning formula for the lost. That formula is God's love for mankind, Jesus.

> FOR GOD SO [GREATLY] LOVED *AND* DEARLY PRIZED THE WORLD, THAT HE [EVEN] GAVE HIS [ONE AND] ONLY BEGOTTEN SON, SO THAT WHOEVER BELIEVES *AND* TRUSTS IN HIM [AS SAVIOR] SHALL NOT PERISH BUT HAVE ETERNAL LIFE… FOR GOD DID NOT SEND HIS SON INTO THE WORLD TO JUDGE *AND* CONDEMN THE WORLD [THAT IS, TO INITIATE THE FINAL JUDGMENT OF THE WORLD], BUT THAT THE WORLD MIGHT BE SAVED THROUGH HIM. (John 3:16–17 AMP, emphasis mine)

The key to enlarging God's kingdom is that the same love shown toward us must now be expressed to those that are outside of the fellowship of God by the believers. The weight of fallen humanity is the believer's, the church's, responsibility. And we must, without excuse, be accountable for failing to do the work assigned to us by God.

Likewise, faithfulness ensures and prepares you for leadership in a world which accept just about all rationale as a solution to problem rather than trusting God. Being available to be used by God at any moment is the key ingredient for upward mobility in any field of endeavor. We all are born with the capacity for leadership, yet some will be trained to undertake this role of accountability for responsibility. The humble in spirit, filled with self-confidence and the courage needed to accomplish any given task, being able to work with others toward the same goals, being able to understand the vision so that it can be communicated to others will always excel to the next dimension of leadership.

The science and art of evangelism is to gain knowledge of the One you are representing so that the desired effect you are expecting from witnessing will be realized in the lives of those whom you share this love story of Jesus the Christ. This work, *THE NEED FOR RAPID DEPLOYMENT IS NOW: BOOTS ON THE GROUND*, is so quintessentially important that failure to implement it properly will result in a life-and-death struggle that will turn us not only against, but, in some cases, to the complete rejection of the God of the Bible and His Word. I employ you, get on up from sitting down. God cannot use you sitting down. The need for rapid for deployment is now, and without a doubt, we need boots on the ground.

Evangelism is team effort. It is a biblical imperative that needs to be undergirded by prayer and fasting. With prayer and fasting as its foundation, along with a team effort, everything you need will fall into place, and your effort to enlarge the kingdom of God will be a success. To God be the glory.

CHAPTER 6

AN ABUNDANCE THAT CANNOT BE DENIED

THEN SAITH HE UNTO HIS DISCIPLES, THE HARVEST
TRULY IS PLENTEOUS, BUT THE LABOURERS ARE FEW.
—Matthew 9:37 (KJV)

The challenge of this chapter is to identify the abundance that Matthew is talking about. During periods of drought, the coronavirus pandemic, and climate change in our world today, where is the abundance, the harvest that cannot be denied? The following information is derived from a Google search.

Looking at the scope of evangelism, which is reaping the harvest for Christ, where is this great harvest that Matthew is speaking of coming from? The following numbers were google-searched from The Pew Research Center. There are 195 countries in the world (Africa = 54, Asia = 48, Europe = 44, Latin America and the Caribbean = 33, Oceania = 14, and Northern America = 2). Of these countries, 193 are members of the United Nations and 2 are nonmembers; they are Holy See and the state of Palestine. Likewise, an additional 3 countries are not included; they are Taiwan, the Cook Islands, and Niue. There are also 50 nations that have declared themselves independent. As of January 20, 2020, the report is that there are 250 countries in the world.

As of September 2020, the current population of the world is 7.8 billion, according to the most recent United Nations estimates. Christianity comprises 2.4 billion; Islam, 1.9 billion; also, Islam is noted as the fastest growing religion and it is set to overtake Christianity by 2070 and become the world's dominant religion; Hinduism, 1.2 billion; Buddhism, 506 million; Judaism, 14.7 million; and 100 million African traditional religions.

I WILL GIVE ONLY A FEW POPULATIONS AS NOTED BY WORLD METER:

COUNTRY	POPULATION	COUNTRY	POPULATION
China	1,439,323,776	Indonesia	273,523,615
India	1,380,004,385	Russia	145,934,462
United States	331,002,651	Mexico	128,932,753

The Pew Research Center Major Religious Groups by percentages: Christianity, 31.4%; Islam, 23.2%; unaffiliated, 16.4%; Hinduism, 15%; Buddhism, 7.1%; folk religions, 5.9%; others, 1.0%.

The breakdown for religions in the United States for 2020:
(The Structure of Religion in the US | Boundless Sociology—Lumen Learning)

The largest religion in the USA is *Christianity*, practiced by most of the population. From those queried, roughly 51.3% of Americans are *Protestants*, 25% are Catholics, 1.7% are *Mormons*, and 1.7% are of various other *Christian* denominations. Northern European peoples introduced *Protestantism*.

Wikipedia's breakdown for religions in the United States (2019):
Protestantism (43%), Catholicism (20%), Mormonism (2%), unaffiliated (26%), Judaism (2%), Islam (1%), Buddhism (1%), Hinduism (1%), other religion (3%), unanswered (2%).

These numbers are reflective of what the Scriptures states in Luke 10:1–4 (AMP):

> NOW AFTER THIS THE LORD APPOINTED SEVENTY OTHERS, AND SENT THEM OUT AHEAD OF HIM, TWO BY TWO, INTO EVERY CITY AND PLACE WHERE HE WAS ABOUT TO GO... HE WAS SAYING TO THEM, THE HARVEST IS ABUNDANT [FOR THERE ARE MANY WHO NEED TO HEAR THE GOOD NEWS ABOUT SALVATION], BUT THE WORKERS [THOSE AVAILABLE TO PROCLAIM THE MESSAGE OF SALVATION] ARE FEW. THEREFORE, [PRAYERFULLY] ASK THE LORD OF THE HARVEST TO SEND OUT WORKERS INTO HIS HARVEST... GO YOUR WAY; LISTEN CAREFULLY: I AM SENDING YOU OUT LIKE LAMBS AMONG WOLVES...DO NOT CARRY A MONEY BELT, A PROVISION BAG, OR [EXTRA] SANDALS; AND DO NOT GREET ANYONE ALONG THE WAY [WHO WOULD DELAY YOU].

This text tells us that the harvest is plenteous and the vision of reaching those that are separated from God in every city, state, nation, and kingdom on the face of this earth can only be realized when we the believers catch the vision and begin to implement it. The harvest is plenteous; therefore, catching the vision and running with it is the key that is so vitally necessary for winning the lost to Christ. The need for rapid deployment is now. Therefore, get on up from sitting down. God cannot use you sitting down. Yes, there is an abundance that cannot be denied. The earth is the Lord's and ALL that dwell therein.

The work and ministry of evangelism is always a team effort, and the success of this effort is based on all team members pulling in the same direction, at the same time, with the same message. That message is Jesus the Christ and Him crucified. Achieving the planned objective gives one a sense of accomplishment and motivation to move forward. When the realization of the kingdom settles in, it not only propels you to do more, but this enthusiasm generates a mindset of a job well done. Remember, if you succeed at and have completed and fulfilled your original goal, certainly, without a doubt, you can do it again and again. The harvest is an abundance that cannot be denied. God with you, possibilities are unlimited.

Failure to complete the task of winning people to Jesus Christ leaves many of us with a defeatist attitude and low self-esteem. With our motivational level sinking to an all-time low have now left us with a negative perspective of ourselves where we have adopted and have become intimately involved with failure's first cousin, the domino effect. And yes, failure can and do, for some, lead to walking away from ministry.

At this point, I think that we need to reflect on the plight of Jeremiah the prophet who ministered for forty years pleading to the people of Judah to repent of their sins with seemingly no positive results.

Judah's behavior was a comparison to the apostle Paul's words as described in 2 Timothy 3:7 (AMP): "ALWAYS LEARNING AND LISTENING TO ANYBODY WHO WILL TEACH THEM, BUT NEVER ABLE TO COME TO THE KNOWLEDGE OF THE TRUTH."

He warned Judah of impending judgment and destruction. Of course, Jeremiah's preaching gendered the hatred of himself by Judah to the point of being beaten and put in stocks. His mindset was to give up and not preach anymore. He became known as "the weeping prophet." This label of him can be viewed as Jeremiah being a weak and an ineffective prophet. Yet his weeping was because of his love for an unrepenting people. Likewise, we today find ourselves in the same situation of doing the will of God, teaching, and preaching day and night, and yet the love of self and all that encompasses a life minus the Creator seem to be the plight of those who reject the call to repentance. The love for the people of God must in all respects surpass whatever you as an individual or group would ever face. Therefore, failure is not an option. You must always remember, everything is about God and His desires for His people. Nothing is about us although we sometimes wish it were.

With a world population of 7.8 billion people and a United States of America population of 331,002,651, and the need for taking this Gospel of Jesus Christ to the world, we can say without a doubt that this is an abundance of souls that cannot be denied hearing the truth of this glorious gospel.

The work of evangelism is not a one- or two-day event; it is a lifetime ministry that will last and continue until the Lord returns for us. We need to develop a program within our churches that is geared toward this objective. Whatever the cost, we need to apprehend our streets and communities if the goal of adding to the church daily is going to be realized. Goals are not obtained unless we are motivated into action now. Therefore, it is extremely important not only to acquaint ourselves with evangelism—by taking courses, attending seminars, going to various evangelical events—but to inculcate within our conscious that this is what the work of the church is all about. Regardless to what the enemy of our lives attempts to do to us, to distract, stop, and hinder us from performing the work assigned to us by God, he is a defeated foe. The text is right: "GREATER IS HE THAT IS IN US THAN HE THAT IS IN THE WORLD."

We need to be noticeably clear about one thing. We cannot effect change in the lives of others until we clean up our own backyard. It is easy to tell others how to live and what to do, but if our own lives are not circumspect before God, we need to do some introspection first and ask God to cleanse and forgive us of our wrongdoing, and then we will be able to help and assist others. Had not God completed a work in our lives first, we would be doomed and consumed by a meaningless and a monotonous existence. However, the transformative power of our Lord and Savior has made us new, and all that is necessary for us to do now is to pass it on. What are we passing on? Simply the love of Jesus Christ.

Jesus was moved with love and compassion at the condition of the lost. He was letting us know that there are plenty of lost souls, but our petty differences concerning who is or is not part of the family of God, which church is the right church, and which domination is commissioned by God, has allowed the enemy to creep in and divide the church into social clubs, entertainment centers, and the work of the church has suffered. There are few believers willing to change their personal agendas for the sake of souls.

Church work is easy, but the work of the church is met with much difficulty because some believers are not willing to change their way of life to increase the kingdom of God. Before we embark on this evangelistic journey of sharing the Gospel message, we must come together with a mind to serve and much prayer. The abundance cannot be denied; however, the laborers are few.

As we share this gospel, we must realize that God has given us dominion, power, and authority over the enemy. Let us catch the vision of evangelism. Evangelism is the core of our expectations for growth and enlargement of the kingdom of God. Its preparation ground begins in the home, our local church. Evangelism is a special and unique way we as believers must deal with those who have chosen an alternative lifestyle as a solution to problem-solving rather than adhering to any religious dogma.

This ministry of evangelism requires to be effective, need capable persons who are willing, ready, and able to deal with the masses of humanity with a global perspective. These persons must be committed to ministry. They without a doubt must know the Word of God as well as putting God first in all situations; and above all, they must have a reverent fear of God. An abundance that cannot be denied speaks to the need of salvation that leads to eternal fellowship with God for all of humanity, and the only way to eternal fellowship with God is through Jesus Christ.

Yes, Jesus is the only way although our personal lifestyles declare, it does not take all that discipline to be saved. Christ taught us that the majority will not follow Him and that only a few, in this mass of humanity, will have a personal accountability of their wrongdoings. We must do all we can to teach and preach this gospel to all. The abundance that cannot be denied is the harvest that needs us now.

CHAPTER 7

NO LOOKING BACK

BUT JESUS SAID TO HIM, NO ONE WHO PUTS HIS HAND
TO THE PLOW AND LOOKS BACK [TO THE THINGS LEFT
BEHIND] IS FIT FOR THE KINGDOM OF GOD.
—Luke 9:62 (AMP)

Now that we have covered all the prerequisites to perform the need for rapid deployment, it is now time to put all that we have learned into practical application. I love the motto of Bread of Life Christian Church and Community Center because it epitomizes the need to put into action all things that have been acquired and is now a part of their lifestyle. The motto states, "LEARNING IS GOOD, APPLICATION IS BETTER." This motto reminds me of the old cliché by the sportswriter Frank Deford that states, "THE PROOF OF THE PUDDING IS IN THE PIE." However, Ben Zimmer stated of this, saying, "THIS IS A NEW TWIST ON A VERY OLD PROVERB. THE ORIGINAL VERSION IS THE PROOF OF THE PUDDING IS IN THE EATING. AND WHAT IT MEANT WAS THAT YOU HAD TO TRY OUT FOOD IN ORDER TO KNOW WHETHER IT WAS GOOD."

I agree with Ben Zimmer. Before you can evangelize the world, you must, without a doubt, do your due diligence first. This necessary work must be done in your local municipalities, states, nations, and then the world. Unless you start at the beginning (home), you will be unable without this experience to go to the next level of winning this world for Christ.

The Bible teaches that charity begins at home and then it spread abroad. This is what I call, as I interpret in my own words, Ben Zimmer's statement, eating the pie is all the proof you need to determine if you are willing to try it again. After you have shared this glorious gospel with others and have seen lives of individuals changed for the better, all you want to do now is tell someone else about Jesus who can change hearts of stones into hearts of flesh. This is based on the change that have taken place in your life first.

The tree is known by the fruit it bears, as declared by Scripture; now you see it in others. The proof of the pudding is in the eating. Listen. We who have been changed by the acceptance of Jesus as Lord and Savior have all the ingredients to make the best pie in the world. What we have to offer—that is, the love of Christ—will excite one's curiosity and create such an appetite that you automatically want more. Read John 1:35–42. In this text, Andrew heard John speak about the Messiah, and his life was changed. Andrew then went and found his brother Simon and brought him to Jesus. There are no reasons to look back after meeting the Messiah because once you meet Jesus, your life will be changed for the better, forever. Second Corinthians 5:17 (AMP) states, "THEREFORE IF ANYONE IS IN CHRIST [THAT IS, GRAFTED IN, JOINED TO HIM BY FAITH IN HIM AS SAVIOR], HE IS A NEW CREATURE [REBORN AND RENEWED BY THE HOLY SPIRIT]; THE OLD THINGS [THE PREVIOUS MORAL AND SPIRITUAL CONDITION] HAVE PASSED AWAY. BEHOLD, NEW THINGS HAVE COME [BECAUSE SPIRITUAL AWAKENING BRINGS A NEW LIFE]." Yes, there are higher heights and deeper depths in Christ, experienced by this acquired new life we have submitted ourselves to, and that we have yearned and longed for.

The farmer must always be mindful of the ground he has just plowed, but also, he must remain focused in and on the completion of his task. Therefore, looking back constantly is an inappropriate response for what lies ahead. Looking ahead requires vision and thought. The ground to be plowed may be filled with all kinds of distractions. That is why remaining focused on the task at hand is key critical to successfully having a good harvest.

There is no looking back. Every day we exist, we experience new and different things. The same issues and situations may be like our previous experiences, but the repeating of the same incidents, as previously done, will never happen. Therefore, it is so important to remain focused and looking forward. Everything that has occurred in the past is only historical data and should be seen and used as a learning experience so that we, hopefully, will not repeat and make those same mistakes again. How does this weigh in juxtaposition to the need for rapid deployment is now? It is quintessentially important not to think that, if someone you are sharing the gospel of Christ with, and knowing some of their personal history, to make a judgment call, saying they are hopeless, and their record indicates that nothing you can say or do will ever change them or their opinion. Remember this: whether they change or not is not your call. The Holy Spirit can and will handle any controversy that you cannot deal with. This is His responsibility. The cliché states, "STAY IN YOUR OWN LANE." Once the Word of God is sown, it is the work of the Holy Spirit to change the thinking and the heart of those whom you have witnessed to. John 16:13–14 (AMP) states, "BUT WHEN HE, THE SPIRIT OF TRUTH, COMES, HE WILL GUIDE YOU UNTO ALL THE TRUTH [FULL AND COMPLETE TRUTH]. FOR HE WILL NOT SPEAK ON HIS OWN INITIATIVE, BUT HE WILL SPEAK WHATEVER HE HEARS [FROM THE FATHER—THE MESSAGE REGARDING HIS SON], AND HE WILL DISCLOSE TO YOU WHAT IS TO COME [IN THE FUTURE]... HE WILL GLORIFY AND HONOR ME, BECAUSE HE (THE HOLY SPIRIT) WILL TAKE FROM WHAT IS MINE AND WILL DISCLOSE IT TO YOU." So then, no looking back keeps us in perspective. We plant and water the seeds; it is the Holy Spirit who changes the heart.

No looking back lets us know that although we base our decision-making on past events, we must be clear that to operate in the "NOW" requires embracing today and tomorrow. Sometimes, we tend to hold on to the things that make us most comfortable, so we end up embracing the past with the hope that the results for today and tomorrow will be different. The values of yesterday have been passed down from generation to generation through tradition. Traditions are good schoolmasters in the learning process. Now we know what to embrace and what to reject. Our focus is to makes our today and tomorrow better. If looking back is not for learning but has become the stable for the "NOW," the Scriptures are needed now more than ever to give us clarity, hope, and purpose. Yes, Luke 9:62 (KJV) states, "AND JESUS SAID UNTO HIM, NO *MAN* HAVING PUTS HIS HAND TO THE PLOUGH, AND LOOKING BACK, IS FIT FOR THE KINGDOM OF GOD."

In the times which we now live, the proclamation of the gospel is the function, or should be, the function of every Christian. Evangelism is a priority, perennial, and a productive work. Enlarging the kingdom of God is an unspeakable joy that can only be experienced personally. Let us remain focused with our fix on the hope of this world. This hope is Jesus the Christ. By being focused, we will discover that there is more ahead of us than behind us; therefore, whatever we attempt to do for kingdom building, let us keep our eyes on our Savior and forward will always be our thrust. No need to look back anymore and trust in yesterday's experiences as the solution for our present and future. Jesus said that He will be with us always. No LOOKING BACK.

CHAPTER 8

LESSON SHEETS ON EVANGELISM

STUDY TO SHEW THYSELF APPROVED UNTO GOD,
A WORKMAN THAT NEEDETH NOT BE ASHAMED,
RIGHTLY DIVIDING THE WORD OF TRUTH.
—2 Timothy 2:15 (KJV)

Evangelism is the art of presenting the gospel of Jesus Christ to enlarge His kingdom on earth.

THREE WAYS TO PRESENT AND IMPLEMENT EVANGELISM

1. *One-on-one*: This is the personal approach. Those to whom you are witnessing is watching your lifestyle. Make sure you are an example of what you preach.
2. *Pastoral*: Once an individual has accepted Christ as their personal Savior, they then need to attach themselves to a Spirit-filled Bible-believing church. This is the place where you can now grow and learn more about the Savior of the world through anointed and Spirit-filled leadership.
3. *Professional*: These are those persons who have been called by God to take this Gospel message to every neighborhood, community, city, state, nation, and the world. *Note*: these

professionals are to present Christ only for the salvation of lost souls. They are not to overstep their area of responsibility and intrude into that of the pastor. The pastors are equipped by God to deal with the multiplicity of needs of the flocks that He has made them overseers of. Although there is a temptation to step into the pastoral role, be careful not to do so, and be very watchful in controlling your enthusiasm for presenting this gospel to others. "ALL THE GLORY BELONGS TO GOD. YOU ARE ONLY AN INSTRUMENT USED BY HIM."

THE OBJECTIVE OF EVANGELISM

1. To have a fisherman's mentality (Matthew 28:19–20, Mark 1:17, 1 Corinthians 9:22–23).
2. To be an ambassador for Christ (Acts 25:14–18, 2 Corinthians 5:20).
3. Share with others what God has done for you (Revelation 12:11).

WHERE AND WHEN DID EVANGELISM BEGIN

1. Origin of the evil tactician (Isaiah 14:12–17, Ezekiel 28:11–19).
2. The fall of man (Genesis 3).
3. The prototype for evangelism (Genesis 3:9, Luke 19:9–10).
4. Purpose of evangelism is to preach and teach Jesus (Matthew 28:19–20).
5. This is a divine undertaking (Acts 8:5–8).
6. The sinful state of man (Psalm 14:3, Jeremiah 17:9, Romans 3:23).

Every believer has the capacity to do this necessary work. They are gifted according to their ability. No gift is more important than the other. They are all given by the same Spirit (1 Corinthians 12).

EDUCATIONAL REQUIREMENTS

1. *Have a working knowledge of the Bible* (2 Timothy 2:15–19).

    a. Where do we find Christ (Psalm 40:7–8, Hebrews 10:5–9).
    b. Be able to compare one truth to another truth (Joshua 24:15).
    c. Some knowledge of theology, sermon preparation, and working with sinners.
    d. Have some knowledge of church history from Judaism to Christianity.

2. *Do some introspection and improve your present ability.*

    a. Have a prayerful life with Christ as your Lord and Savior. Be an example.
    b. You need a knowledge of current events:

        1. newspapers/commentaries
        2. magazines/dictionaries
        3. television/radio
        4. social media

    c. Learning is good, application is better (2 Timothy 1:3–7).
    d. Seek understanding (Proverbs 4:7) and be led by the Holy Spirit (John 16:13).

3. *Reconnaissance: know whom you are ministering to and the location you must travel to:*

    a. home
    b. streets/your neighborhood, community, city, state
    c. hospitals

    d.   nursing homes, youth facilities
    e.   schools
    f.   colleges
    g.   prisons
    h.   foreign lands, nations, and the world
    i.   wherever the need is

EVANGELISTIC QUALIFICATIONS

1. Be noticeably clear about whom you are serving by having a made-up mind (Romans 1:16).

   a. Realization of the holiness of God (Exodus 15:11, Leviticus 11:45).
   b. Be consciousness of the power of the cross (1 Corinthians 1:17–31).
   c. Know that man is sinful (Genesis 6:5).

2. Not only do you love Christ, but you must have a deep love for fallen humanity (Jeremiah 9:1).
3. Must have a capacity for leadership (Matthew 16:17–23).

YOU MUST HAVE AN UNMISTAKABLE ASSURANCE THAT GOD HAS CALLED YOU TO THIS WORK.

Clarity of purpose will conflict with everything else that you, the individual, undertakes until it is confessed. First Corinthians 9:16 (AMP) states, "FOR IF I [MERELY] PREACH THE GOSPEL], I HAVE NOTHING TO BOAST ABOUT, FOR I AM COMPELLED [THAT IS, ABSOLUTELY OBLIGATED TO DO IT]. WOE TO ME IF I DO NOT PREACH THE GOOD NEWS [OF SALVATION]!"

PROOF OF AN EVANGELISTIC EXPERIENCE

John 6:35–40 talks about the wonderful change taking place in the life of nonbelievers who for the first time experience the salvific change through the shed blood of Jesus Christ. As mentors of these new babes in Christ, when these new babes *see* preaching (by the lifestyle of the believer) and *hearing* words of faith only when necessary, immediately they begin to order their lives, not because of what the Scriptures says but by observing the example before them. The more they observed, the greater their faith walk begin to increase to the point that it does not matter what the mentor will do at some point later, right or wrong. Their hope in God has now become the foundation of their lives, and they will now declare as the song which is attributed to Sadhu Sundar Singh, an Indian missionary, and composed by William Jensen Reynolds, an American hymn editor, "I HAVE DECIDED TO FOLLOW JESUS, NO TURNING BACK, NO TURNING BACK."

EVANGELISTIC DUE DILIGENCE

Along with evangelistic qualifications, organize based on the following:

1. Make sure you do background checks on all Christian workers.
2. Groups organized according to: *youth, young adults, adults, senior citizens*, etc. Assign appropriate persons to each group based on their background and qualifications.
3. Be ready to do street ministry, door-to-door visitations as well as various community programs.
4. Prepare workers for alter work, counseling, follow up on those ministered to, and establish various prayer groups.
5. Marketing and statistical analysis groups. Record-keeping is extremely important.
6. Literature committees.

Epilogue

As we view the landscape of our earthly existence, survival of the fittest seems to be the mantra by which we sustain ourselves. Our survival, without any outside stimulus, is solely based on self-sufficiency. In this life, if you are concerned with yourself only, it is most likely that you will not progress to the maximum of your potential. This is a selfish way of thinking because it divorces you from interaction with others. We do not live in this world alone. The needs of others and their contributions toward your destiny are crucial for your personal survival.

This book is a survival kit, a motivational tool to aid in helping you find the right solution in the realization of an escape route from a mundane and monotonous lifestyle. This book serves as a tool which inevitably will push you, me, and all others into their purpose. God's love for us is the cause that drives us and keeps us focused on our task of evangelizing the world and claiming every town, county, city, state, and nation for the kingdom of God. The hope is to guide everyone we reach to a place of stability, prosperity, and upward mobility.

As we look at the conditions of today, the new normalcy is today's reality. This will not change. From this day forward, the coronavirus pandemic, systematic racism and injustice, police brutality, unequal opportunities in housing, employment, and in education have altered our way of living and thinking so much that we are now looking for new ways to achieve our goals, particularly, the growth of God's kingdom. This altering has forced some of us into this digital world of communicating that we at one time thought would be contrary to the work of the Lord. Yet it has caused us to take advantage of every opportunity (CARPE DIEM—"SEIZE THE DAY"), and with preciseness and exactness, we have been able to now operate in foreign venues that we the ignorant thought was impossible. How quickly do we forget Luke 1:37 (KJV): "FOR WITH GOD NOTHING SHALL BE IMPOSSIBLE"? It is also noteworthy at this point to also quote Philippians 4:13 (KJV): "I CAN DO ALL THINGS THROUGH CHRIST WHICH STRENGTHENETH ME."

We have been commissioned to go into all the world and share this glorious gospel of Jesus the Christ. What faster way of accomplishing this mandate than to use the available tools already provided: Facebook, Instagram, Zoom, webinar, and other sources. We have no excuse in fulfilling this task of world evangelism. Certainly, we cannot progress in Christ, nor in this society, if we are steadfastly looking back and desiring that which will never be again. Yesterday is gone and will not return. What then is the new normalcy? We need to take each day, one day at a time, and never forget that God is still in charge. It does not matter what the climate of today is; the Lord has given us the ability to ambulate through each experience of the day. Trusting God to be with us is always a guaranteed victory. We always respond to yesterday's events to determine our future aspirations. So then, yesterday is only historical data and it will never return. We must use the past as our springboard for today and tomorrow. In this life, whenever tomorrow shows up, it is always today. Therefore, we must occupy in this moment of today and prepare for our tomorrow experience, with or without the Lord Jesus Christ. Therefore, evangelism, or should I say, boots on the ground, is a necessary work for the Christian community.

With clarity of purpose, we know that evangelism is not about us; it is about Christ and His purpose for mankind. We understand that to effectuate this ministry on a global scale, we need a unified effort, a team functioning as a unit with one objective, winning the lost at any cost. This will let Satan know that all efforts on his part to destroy the work of Christ in the lives of men and women are futile.

The need for rapid deployment is now. The kingdom of heaven can only be taken hold of by forceful people who are committed to breaking away from the sinful and immoral practices of mankind and by those who turn to Christ, His Word, and His righteous ways.

The kingdom is not for those who seldom pray and compromise with the world, and certainly, the kingdom is not for those who neglect the Word and do not thirst for the ways of Christ. We must now resolve, if we expect to maximize our efforts in kingdom building, teamwork is the key. Working together, we will have greater power. However, trying to do this work alone, we will have greater battles. Never ever forget, the battle is the Lord's. He is always the winner; we are just His tools.

References

Bibles

1. Amplified Bible
2. King James Version and the New King James Version
3. New Living Translation
4. The Book by Tyndale House Publishers, Inc.
5. Life in the Spirit Study Bible (King James Version)

Books

1. Dr. Myles Munroe. *The Spirit of Leadership, Understanding the Purpose and Power of Prayer, and The Pursuit of Purpose.*
2. Kevin Conner and Ken Malmin. *Interpreting the Scriptures.*
3. Perry Stone. *There's a Crack in Your Armor.*
4. John McArthur. *The Truth War.*
5. Charles Capp. *God's Image of You.*
6. Darrell W. Robinson. *People Sharing Jesus.*

Music

1. The Late Rev. Timothy Wright. "Get on Up from Sitting Down, God Can't Use You Sitting Down."
2. Buddy Greene and Jeff Taylor. "Denomination Blues, the Last Stanza."
3. Garo, Assam (renewaljournal.com). "I Have Decided to Follow Jesus, No Turning Back."
4. Ronald and Equila Wright. "Ringing Doorbells for my Lord."

Quotes

1. Frank Deford: "The proof of the pudding is in the pie."
2. Ben Zimmer: "The proof of the pudding is in the eating."

Web

Google Search: vocabulary.com, the bibleref.com, renewalpurnal.com. The Pew Research Center.

ABOUT THE AUTHOR

Dr. James R. Davis is the pastor of Bread of Life Christian Church, Inc. and the president of New Covenant Bible Institute, Inc., organized respectively in New York City in 1992 and in Rocky Mount, North Carolina, in 1996.

On May 19, 2009, New Covenant Bible Institute, Inc. was granted accreditation status by the American Accrediting Association of Theological Institutions, Inc. On December 10, 2012, Dr. Davis was appointed to the planning board for the city of Rocky Mount, North Carolina. His credentials as a Christian scholar are widely known within the Christian and non-Christian communities to whom he interfaces with daily, and his personal background has given him a unique perspective on the Christian life.

Dr. Davis was born in Rocky Mount, North Carolina, and relocated to New York City with his parents in 1954. He served in the United States Army as a medical corpsman from 1965 to 1968, receiving the good conduct medal and numerous letters of accommodation for his service and performance. He received his bachelor of arts degree in sociology from Brooklyn College, Brooklyn, New York, in 1975, and his bachelor's and master's degrees respectively in 1987 and 1988 in general Bible and religious education from the United Christian College of the United Holy Church of America in New York City. The doctor of sacred theology degree was conferred on him in 1989, also from the United Christian College of the United Holy Church of America in New York City.

Dr. Davis's infectious personality allows him to exemplify the Word of God in his everyday life. On most occasions, you will find him working to help improve the lives of those in his community as well as the surrounding communities. Whether he is in board rooms or attending to the needs of impoverished persons, Dr. Davis's ministry is fixated on following the examples given in the Word of God. He is married to his lovely wife, Lorraine (Lady) Sutrina Davis, of fifty-five years. They have two sons, two wonderful daughters-in-love, five grandchildren, and two great-grandchildren.

Dr. Davis has adopted his brother Bishop George W. Davis II's motto as his model to live by: "IT's A PLEASURE TO SERVE, AND ANYTHING LESS THAN MY BEST IS A SIN."

CPSIA information can be obtained
at www.ICGtesting.com
Printed in the USA
JSHW031930080622
26872JS00003B/9